— WHO IS BOB RICHARDSON?
BORN IN BROOKLYN ON JAN 3, 1928
IRISH CATHOLIC FAMILY — GREW
UP ON LONG ISLAND — LARGE HOUSE
SIX CHILDREN — DOGS — CATS & BIRDS,
MY PARENTS NEVER FALTERED —
WE WERE TAUGHT HARD WORK
PLUS AMBITION PLUS IRISH LUCK
WOULD SEE US THROUGH — 1928
WAS THE YEAR OF THE "GREAT
DEPRESSION" — BUT MY FATHER
PROSPERED — IT WAS ALSO
PROHIBITION — EVERY NIGHT MY
PARENTS HAD TWO MARTINIS BEFORE
DINNER — POURED FROM AN ART
DECO COCKTAIL SHAKER.

50's ONE MORNING IN THE EARLY 50's
I WOKE UP IN THE PSYCHO ~~PSYCHO~~ WARD
AT BELLEVUE HOSPITAL — MY
STOMACH HAD BEEN PUMPED
OF BIG AMOUNT OF BARBITURATES —
I HAD ONLY VAGUE MEMORY OF
SWALLOWING THEM — THIS WAS THE
FIRST OF FOUR SUICIDE ATTEMPTS.
IT TAKES COURAGE TO LIVE — AND
COURAGE TO DIE — I WAS IN LIMBO —

- "GREAT AND SMALL — FUCK 'EM ALL." — IRISH QUOTE WHEN YOU ARE 75 YOU WILL UNDERSTAND.

- PARIS EARLY 60'S —
  IN ST. CLOUD — OUTSIDE PARIS — THERE'S A SANATARIUM THAT OFFER A "SLEEPING CURE" — WITHDRAWING FROM A FOUR YEAR AMPHETAMINE HABIT WAS MADE BEARABLE BY SLEEPING THROUGH NIGHTMARISH WITHDRAWAL —
  DR. PIERRE BENSOUSAN WORKED WITH CREATIVE PEOPLE — HE WOULD GIVE ME SODIUM PENTATHOL SO THAT I COULD SPEAK TO HIM —

- 90'S NEW YORK —
  TOTAL NY.COM WEBSITE CARRIES A PIECE ON ME WITH VOICE OVER AND ANNIE LENNOX MUSIC.

- 2000 NEW YORK.
  TWO DIRECTORS IN MUNICH + ONE DIRECTOR IN LONDON INTERESTED IN DOCUMENTING MY LIFE — CONT.

① ~~"WHICH ONE ARE YOU"~~ OUTSIDER
"~~PHOENIX~~ ~~OUTSIDER~~
~~BOB IZHARD~~"

- F. SCOTT FITZGERALD SAID THERE ARE NO SECOND ACTS IN AMERICAN LIVES — BULL SHIT.

- APRIL 3, 1997 — STALEY WEISS GALLERY IN SOHO — COMEBACK EXHIBITION TITLED "BEYOND COOL" — COVERED & REVIEWED BY NEW YORK MEDIA INCLUDING N.B.C. TELEVISION —

- "DATELINE N.B.C." SEGMENT COVERING THIS SECOND ACT, ESTIMATED VIEWERSHIP AT TWENTY MILLION AMERICANS —

- "E ENTERTAINMENT T.V. INTERVIEW

- THREE THOUSAND WORD ARTICLE IN TINA BROWN'S "NEW YORKER" MAGAZINE — ANNOUNCING COMEBACK

- FOURTY PAGES OF PHOTOGRAPHS FOR COMEBACK ISSUE ITALIAN VOGUE L'UOMO MEN'S MAGAZINE —

- TEACHING PHOTOGRAPHY CLASS AT SCHOOL OF VISUAL ARTS - NEW YORK CITY.

- TOO POOR TO OWN A CAMERA - I BORROWED ONE.

- WHY WRITE MY AUTOBIOGRAPHY - BIG EGO ? HELP YOUNG PEOPLE ? TRY BOTH.

- THANKS TO ELECTRO-SHOCK THERAPY MY MEMORY FOR DATES IS GONE - VIVIDLY RECALL DECADES.

- PUBLICITY ABOUT ME POINTS TO SEX - DRUGS + ROCK + ROLL AS THE REASON FOR MY DISAPEERANCE FOR FIFTEEN YEARS - MORE BULL SHIT. AT AGE 22 I WAS DIAGNOSED AS PARANOID SCHITZOFRENIC - A DARK TERRIFYING WORLD WELCOMED ME - DOCTORS FEEL IF YOU CAN SURVIVE TO OLD AGE YOU CAN LEAVE THIS INSANITY - I AM 75 YEARS OLD.

- TWO DIRECTORS IN L.A. WANTING TO DO A FEATURE FILM ON MY LIFE - TWO ACTORS (ONE ENGLISH + ONE AMERICAN) INTERESTED - BECAUSE ALL OF THESE DIRECTORS WERE FIXATED ON SEX - DRUGS - ROCK + ROLL + NOT ~~ON~~ ON MY LIFE - THE ANSWER WAS NO - WAS OFFERED GOOD MONEY FOR MY PARTICIPATION AND AS ALLWAYS I WAS BROKE.

- 30'S LONG ISLAND
TOOK A LOOK AT MY FIRST GRADE CLASSMATES - THE BULLIES AND THE COWARDS - STARTED MAKING MY OWN WORLD - SEEKING GOD - VERY YOUNG CHILDREN ARE CONSTANTLY RECORDING - LIES ARE EASY - TRUTH PAINFULL - YOU DON'T CHOOSE AS A CHILD - YOU PLAY THE CARDS YOU'RE DEALT -

- 60'S NEW YORK -
DOCTOR FEELGOOD TURNED ME ON TO MAINLINING SPEED - TRIPPING 24 HOURS A DAY - WAITING ROOM

WITH ANXIOUS PATIENTS — (BOB DYLAN — TRUMAN CAPOTE — TENNESSEE WILLIAMS —) BIG RUMOR HAS DOCTOR JAKE TREATING JACK KENNEDY. MY LIMO ~~DIES~~ JOINING OTHERS BETWEEN 5TH + MADISON — ARMS COVERED WITH TRACK MARKS. NEEDED CHAMPAGNE + WEED TO LEVEL OUT. UP ALL NIGHT EDITING FILM + LISTENING TO MUSIC — ME + MY DOG "LUCKY" —

— PARIS 60'S
COCO CHANEL ENCOUNTER ON RUE CAMBON — BEAUTIFUL CLOTHES — CIGARETTE HANGING FROM HER MOUTH — SUPERB TASTE. NOW LOST FOREVER. SHE TELLS ME MY STETSON IS NICE — SHE ADDRESSED ME IN ENGLISH — I ANSWERED IN FRENCH — THINK OF THE FORTUNES PLAGIARISTS HAVE MADE OFF THIS ORIGINAL'S TALENT. THEY DON'T MAKE THEM LIKE THAT ANYMORE —

— EARLY 60'S —
HARPER'S BAZAAR DISCOVERED

ME + DIANE ARBUS — POWERFUL + DIFFICULT ART DIRECTOR MARVIN ISRAEL + FASHION EDITOR DIANA VREELAND — YOU HAD TO BE AN ORIGINAL — RETAKES ORDERED TILL YOU GOT IT RIGHT — FIERCELY COMPETITIVE DICK AVEDON STUDYING MY PHOTOGRAPHS IN THE ART DEPARTMENT — EDITORS LIVING IN THE PAST — UNAWARE OF 60'S ROCK + SHOCK REVOLUTION — DIANE'S WORK KILLED AS TOO WIERD — MINE AS TOO STRONG — TOO REAL — TOO SEXUAL — KEY WORD "GROOVIE" — EVENTUALLY AVEDON — ARBUS — RICHARDSON QUIT — THEY NEVER REPLACED US — THERE ARE LEADERS AND FOLLOWERS — WHICH ONE ARE YOU ?? —

— 2003 — LA LA LAND — THE "STARS" ARE EMBEDDED IN HOLLYWOOD BLVD. CONCRETE WHERE TOURISTS WALK ALL OVER THEM + STRAY DOGS PISS ON THEM — LATE AT NIGHT OUT COME THE TRAMP — THE VAMP — THE ~~CAMP~~ — THE CAMP — SCAMP

— MID 30'S — THANK GOD FOR SISTER FRANCE REGINA THE KIND NUN — THE ONLY ONE WHO SMELLED CLEAN — TWO HOURS OF HOMEWORK EVERY NIGHT — IF YOU FAILED YOU WERE KEPT BACK — IF YOU MISBEHAVED A RULER CAME DOWN ON YOUR KNUCKLES — WE LEARNED — THE MOTHER SUPERIOR TERRIFIED ALL OF US — LONG LIVE SAINT AGNES ACADEMY —

— MID 60'S — SANTA MONICA BEACH — DRUNK & DIRTY — ROUSTED BY THE POLICE BECAUSE A MAN WAS STANDING OVER ME WITH A BREAD KNIFE — WALK ALL NIGHT & SLEEP DURING DAYTIME — MY BEST FRIENDS WERE EARNEST & JULIO GALLO AND THEIR CONTRIBUTION TO ALL BUMS — "WHITE PORT" — A CHEAP NARCOTIC — TWO YEARS OF DARKNESS & TERROR — JAIL TIME FOR STEALING A BLANKET. ONE DAY I AWOKE TO FIND A BAR OF SOAP AND A CLEAN TOWEL NEXT TO MY HEAD —

— MID 60'S ACAPULCO.
BIG SCANDAL — LANA TURNER &
JOHNNY STOMPANATO HAVING MARATHON
SEX AT FULL VOLUME IN THEIR
BUNGALO AT TEDDY STAUFFER'S
HOTEL — BEAUTIFUL BAR IN THE
CENTER OF THE POOL — DRINKING
MARGARITAS IN WASTE DEEP
WATER — WEED CALLED "ACAPULCO
GOLD" EVERYWHERE — DISCOTEQUE
IN THE MIDDLE OF AN OIL FIELD —
BORROWED UNDERWATER NIKON FROM
JACQUES CUSTEAU — PHOTOGRAPHED
CLOTHES ON MODEL UNDERWATER —
A SILENT DANGEROUS PARADISE —
ALL THE CLOTHES DESTROYED —
PHOTOS WERE PUBLISHED BECAUSE
THIS LOCATION TRIP COST —

— MID 30'S — CATHEDRAL AS SANCTUARY —
CHILDREN LEARN TO READ —
I READ TO LEARN —
THE SMALL UGLY ST. AGNES
CATHEDRAL ON LONG ISLAND,
SCHOOLS OUT 3 P.M. AVOIDING
THE BULLY GAUNTLET + SEEKING
SAFETY — ASKING GOD ON MY KNEES
FOR GUIDANCE — 3:30 ALL CLEAR —

THREE MILE BICYCLE RIDE HOME, LAST PART OF JOURNEY THROUGH WOODS — NO FEAR HERE — WATCHING THE BIRDS AND THEIR GRACEFUL FREEDOM — THE NUNS ARE CERTAIN SINFUL CHILDREN ARE PUNISHED — NOT THE BULLY — JUST THE PREY — HE IS NOT MY GOD — TEARS NEVER COME — YOU ARE SAFE ALONE — YOU CAN DREAM —

MID 60'S ROME — TORLONIA PALACE OFF VIA NAZIONALI — PHOTOGRAPH ITALIAN COUTURE FOR HARPER'S BAZAAR — PRINCE TORLONIA TAKES ME THROUGH PALACE BUILT AROUND PERFECT COURTYARD — HE + HIS SISTER ON THEIR WAY TOWARD "RICH HIPPYVILLE" — THE PENTHOUSE RENTED TO KAY TOMPSON WHO PLAYS A GRAND PIANO WITH THE LEGS CUT OFF — PHOTOGRAPH DEBORAH DIXON (MICK JAGGER'S) GIRL — THE EDITOR CALLS ANNA MANGANI'S BOYFRIEND TO POSE — HE'S BEAUTIFUL + VERY YOUNG. THE CITY — THE PEOPLE — THE FOOD BLOW ME AWAY — MY FAVORITE PLACE IN EUROPE! —

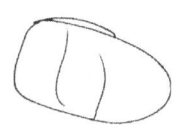

→ LATE 30's — THE JAPANESE SAY REVENGE IS A CATHARSIS — USING MY OLDER BROTHER'S BASEBALL BAT AGAINST THE NEIGHBORHOOD BULLY FRIGHTENS HIM — A LESSON LEARNED — ONE DAY IN THE 80's I WOULD USE A KNIFE TO FRIGHTEN MY OLDER BROTHER — A LESSON FOR HIM —

→ EARLY 60's — JILL KENNINGTON — ENGLISH MODEL — SENSATIONAL BEAUTY — LOVE AT FIRST SIGHT — WE WORKED IN NEW YORK — LONDON — PARIS — VENICE — SHE CAME TO MY STUDIO WITH HER BOYFRIEND OF THE MOMENT — HE THREATENED ME WITH A GUN & FIRED TWO SHOTS INTO THE STUDIO CEILING. NEVER SAW HIM AGAIN — WE WORKED IN EAST HAMPTON WHERE I INSISTED ON PHOTOGRAPHING HER WITHOUT MAKEUP — I AM STILL IN LOVE WITH HER — SHE'S NOW A PHOTOGRAPHER — SHE WAS 60's MOD WITH MINI SKIRTS & BOOTS — SHE COULD KNOCK BACK A LOT OF BOOZE!

- MID 30'S – EVERY SATURDAY MY FATHER WOULD DRIVE THE FOUR OF US TO COFESSION – I ALLWAYS MADE UP SINS – & ALLWAYS RECEIVED THE SAME PENNANCE. THE PRIEST SMELLED FROM SACRIFICIAL WINE – SEEMED BORED – EVERY SUNDAY MORNING THE WHOLE FAMILY WENT TO 9 AM MASS + COMMUNION – THEY PASSED THE COLLECTION PLATE TWICE – WE HAD BREAKFAST "OUT" IN CHURCH – CANDELS – FLOWERS – INCENSE – ORGAN MUSIC – PURE SHOW BUISNESS – PRIEST I EXPENSIVE VESTMENTS ASKING FOR MONEY – ALLWAYS THE POOR – HOW MUCH ACTUALLY GOT TO THEM – THEY'LL NEVER TELL –

= MID 70'S – HOMELESS IN SANTA MONICA – I SLEPT ON CHURCH STEPS FOR SAFETY – ONE NIGHT THE PRIEST CALLED POLICE + HAD ME MOVED – HE STOOD INSIDE THE DOOR WHERE HE HAD A WARM – SAFE HOME – WOULD JESUS WHO WAS BORN HOMELESS HAVE CALLED POLICE WITH RIOT BATONS –

— WRITING THIS IS DIFFICULT — ANGER HELPED ME THRU ALL THE CHAOS — I AM A HUMBLE MAN WHO IS PROUD OF HIMSELF — FIGHTING BACK IS BETTER THAN ANY DRUG — ANY HIGH — THERE ARE HEROS + COWARDS — WHICH ONE ARE YOU —

— 30's
— I GREW UP IN A LARGE HOUSE IN A SMALL TOWN — MY FATHER HAD THE ATTIC FINISHED + MY BROTHER BUDDY + I SHARED TWIN BEDS + TWIN DESKS — IT WAS HOT IN SUMMER + COLD IN WINTER — THE WINDOWS OPEN BECAUSE FRESH AIR IS GOOD FOR YOU — EVERY NIGHT A TRAIN WENT THROUGH TOWN ON IT'S WAY TO MONTAUK — THE TRAIN'S WISTLE WAS SO FAR AWAY — IN THE WINTER MILK WAS DELIVERED BY HORSE + SLEIGH — PROGRESS PUT AN END TO THAT — WORLD WAR 2 PUT AN END TO AN ENTIRE AMERICAN DREAM — MAYBE TO AMERICA PERIOD —

(14)

EARLY 60'S
— MADRID AND LOVE FOR CHILDREN —
GENIUS & SCHIZOPHRENIA ARE
OFTEN IDENTICAL TWINS —
(VINCENT VAN ~~GOGH~~ — EZRA POUND.)
MOZART ALLWAYS ~~DRUNK~~
COCTEAU ADORED ~~MORPHINE~~ OPIUM
IN MADRID'S PARK THE DUCHESS
OF ALBA (DRESSED LIKE PEASANT)
SHOWS ME A ROOM HUNG WITH
EL GRECO PORTRAITS OF HER ANCESTORS —
ANOTHER ROOM ALL VELASQUEZ —
BEAUTIFUL PALACE — BEAUTIFUL
CREATURE — IT TAKES ONE TO KNOW ONE —
PHOTOGRAPHED 3 YOUNG AMERICAN
CHILDREN IN DRAWING ROOM —
TOOK KIDS & EDITOR BY CAR SOUTH
TO THE COSTA DEL SOL — PROUD OF
THESE PICTURES — THE CHILDREN
MESMERISED BY ME — TAKES ONE
TO KNOW ONE — THIS WAS MY FIRST
~~INSTALL~~ ASSIGNMENT FOR HARPER'S
BAZAAR — CHILDREN'S MOM IS MRS.
HENRY LUCE & ONE OF THE GIRLS IS
SCHIZOPHRENIC —

— THE NUNS TOLD US THAT IF WE

WERE GOOD WE WOULD GO TO HEAVAN (ST. PETER AS THE DOORMAN) IF WE WERE BAD WE WOULD BURN IN HELL — HAVING LIVED FOR A YEAR ON EVERY STREET IN HELL THE NUNS WERE WRONG — FIRE IS SO FAST — SUFFERING CAN LAST A LIFETIME — THE WAY TO TEACH CHILDREN IS TO TELL THEM THE TRUTH — PERIOD WHY DO NUNS WANT TO LIVE WITH OTHER WOMEN AND NOT WITH MEN — WHY DON'T THEY WANT THEIR OWN CHILDREN ONE WONDERS — WHAT ARE THEIR SECRETS — EVERYONE HAS SECRETS —

— DANGER FASCINATED ME IN MID 60's — PHOTOGRAPHED IN HOVERING HELICOPTERS — YOU SIT IN OPER DOOR — WITH AN ASSISTANT HOLDING MY BELT FROM BEHIND — SHOOTING DOWN BETWEEN MY LEGS — HOVERING OVER SURFERS GIRLS IN JEEP — PHOTOGRAPHED MODEL SARAH LOWNDES ON HARLEY DAVIDSON IN BLACK LEATHER — TEARING

THROUGH CENTRAL PARK AT 6 AM — WHEN WE WERE DONE SHE TOLD ME SHE HAD NEVER DRIVEN A BIKE — SHE LATER MOVED TO WOODSTOCK & MARRIED BOB DYLAN — RECENTLY PHOTOGRAPHED HER SON JACOB DYLAN —

= MID 80's — WHEN MY FATHER DIED WE FOUND IN HIS SAFE A MEDAL HE HAD BEEN AWARDED IN WORLD WAR I — IN THE ARGONNE FORREST HE WAS MACHINE GUNNED THROUGH BOTH THIGHS BY THE GERMANS — AMERICA WAS LIBERATING FRANCE HE WAS HUNG ON BARBED WIRE FOR 24 HOURS TILL MEDICS COULD REACH HIM — EVACUATED TO ENGLAND WHERE THE SISTERS FORCED HIM TO WALK — TO DANCE — TO SWIM — HE DISCOVERED ~~THE~~ ROSE GARDENS IN THE COUNTRESIDE — HE DIED WORKING IN HIS OWN ROSE GARDEN — HE WAS A LIFELONG ANGLOPHILE — HE IS THE ONLY REAL MAN I HAVE EVER ~~HAVE~~ KNOWN — I THINK OF HIM EVERY DAY & I LOOK EXACTLY LIKE HIM —

- ~~EARLY 60'S - MY TREADMILL.~~

- SOME OF THE BEST POETRY WRITTEN IN MY LIFETIME ARE ROCK +ROLL LYRICS - MOST OF THE DULLEST POETRY HAS BEEN WRITTEN BY THE POETS -

- EARLY 60'S - MY TREADMILL - MODEL'S RUNNING ON AN OLD OPERA CO.'S MACHINE - WIND MACHINE BLOWING CLOTHES + HAIR - CROPPED OUT TREADMILL - PEOPLE FLOATING THROUGH THE AIR TOWARD CAMERA - PUT BARYSHNIKOV RUNNING - TRYING TO LOOK BEAUTIFUL - UNABLE TO DO HIS DIVA ROUTINE - LATER I SHOT PEOPLE ON HUGHE TRAMPOLINE - FLOATING TOWARD CLOUDS ABOVE THEM - HOW PROPHETIC - EASTMAN KODAK SENT PHOTOGRAPHS ON WORLD WIDE MUSEUM TOUR -

- MY MOTHER WAS BORN MARY ELIZABETH MCCOY - TALL + RAIN -

BEAUTIFUL POSTURE - WHEN YOUNG SHE HAD RED HAIR + GREEN EYES + A HOT TEMPER - EVERY SCHOOL MORNING IN THE BREAKFAST ROOM SHE TOLD HER CHILDREN HER DREAMS - VERY SUPERSTICIOUS - EVERYTHING WAS A SIGN TO HER - DRINKING COFFEE + SMOKING PALL MALLS - WHEN WE LEFT FOR SCHOOL SHE WOULD TELL US TO STAND UP STRAIGHT. SHE CALLED EACH OF US "DARLING" -

— 60'S ADVERTISING -
HAD TO MEET CHARLES REVSON AT REVLON - AFTER LOOKING AT MY PHOTOGRAPHS HE SAID "I'M TOLD YOU'RE A GENIUS BUT I DON'T SEE IT" - I REPLIED "GET YOUR EYES EXAMINED" - SLAMMED THE DOOR BEHIND ME - SIX MONTHS LATER SHOT AN AD ON LAUREN HUTTON - THE BEST AGENCY ON MADISON AV. WAS DOYLE DANE BERNBACK - DID A LOT OF CAMPAINS FOR THEM - GOOD YOUNG ART DIRECTORS TRYING TO BE "GROOVIE" -

- LATE 30'S
EVERY CHILD IS SEXUALLY CURIOUS. IF NOTHING IS EXPLAINED TO THEM THEY ARE CONFUSED - TALKING TO CHILDREN ABOUT SEX WAS TABOO FOR MY GENERATION - I ASSUME MY PARENTS HOPED WE WOULD FIND OUT ABOUT SEX AND NOT BRING UP THE SUBJECT AT THE DINNER TABLE. I REMEMBER MY OLDER BROTHER TELLING ME THAT TOO MUCH MASTURBATION COULD HARM YOU - HOW UNCOOL IS THAT.

- EARLY 60'S - PARIS
DIANE VON FURSTENBERG (MRS. BARRY DILLER) WAS MY AGENT IN PARIS. SHE IS BEAUTIFUL + INTELIGENT. IT MUST BE HARD AS HELL CLIMBING IN HIGH HEELS. HER PARTNER (ALBERT KOSKI) FLED TO MEXICO WITH PHOTOGRAPHER'S MONEY - HIS GIRLFRIEND WAS SECOND STRING MODEL GRACE CODDINGTON FROM LONDON.

2003 — L.A.
– MY SON TERRY TOLD ME THAT UNSIGNED PRINTS OF MINE ARE FOR SALE ON THE INTERNET — THESE PRINTS WERE STOLEN — I AM AS USUAL — FLAT BROKE & SOMEONE IS MAKING MONEY FROM MY TALENT —

– 2008 L.A. — STANLEY KUBRICK WHO LIVED & WORKED IN ENGLAND WAS QUOTED AS SAYING THAT HOLLYWOOD IS MALEVELANT —

– MID 30'S — ONE CHRISTMAS MY PARENTS GIFT WAS AN EASLE — CANVAS ~~CANVAS~~ BOARD~~S~~ & A LARGE BOX (MADE OF WOOD IN ENGLAND) — THIS MAGIC BOX FILLED WITH EXQUISITE WINDSOR & NEWTON OIL PAINTS — BRUSHES — KNIFE — PALETTE — TURPENTINE — I LOVE THE SMELLS — SOMETIMES I GO INTO AN ART SUPPLY STORE JUST TO SEE WHAT THEY DISPLAY — HOW WONDERFUL THAT MY PARENTS DID THIS — MY OLDER BROTHER'S

GIFTS WERE ALL BASEBALL EQUIPMENT (CLASSIC BAT - GLOVE) I DON'T RECALL WHAT MY SISTER JOAN RECEIVED - I MADE A STUDIO UNDER A WINDOW IN THE BASEMENT NEAR THE HUGE OIL BURNER - WHEN I RAN OUT OF CANVAS BOARD I PAINTED ON WOOD - I PAINTED BIRDS & FLOWERS ON A MILK BOTTLE - FINALLY I HAD A HOME I LOVED - THANKYOU GOD - I THOUGHT THAT AN ARTIST WAS A PAINTER - I LEARNED LATER ON THAT ANY ENDEAVOR WHERE ONE WORKED WITH ONE'S IMAGINATION WAS AN ART FORM - A CRAFT - A GIFT FROM GOD.

> 60'S - BECOMING ONE OF A SMALL GROUP OF PHOTOGRAPHERS CALLED "JET SET" - AND FUELED BY SPEED - TRAVEL WAS A TRIP - LIMO TO KENNEDY - SKY CAP GRABS BAGS - ASSISTANT CARRYING OLD LOUIS VUITON CAMERA BAG - TWO GIN & TONICS IN AIRPORT LOUNGE - BOARD WITH FIRST CLASS AISLE SEAT -

IN FLIGHT CHAMPAGNE & VALIUM TO KILL THE EDGE — NEVER TAKE OFF SHADES — ARRIVE HEATHROW OR ORLY — CHAUFFER WAITING AT GATE HOLDING SIGN "RICHARDSON" — TIME FOR LATE DINNER WITH MODEL — BACK TO HOTEL & BED — SOMETIMES ALONE — NEXT DAY BEAT JET LAG WITH A SHOT IN MY ASS OF B12 + SOME SPEED — CLOTHES FROM "GRANNIE TAKES A TRIP" STORE ON KING'S ROAD + FROM ARMY-NAVY STORE ON 14 STREET —

= 60'S — LIVING ON SPEED YOUR JAWS GRIND — YOU CAN'T SHUT UP — + YOU SWEAT — EVEN HASH OR WEED WON'T CUT IT — REMEMBER SEEING EXTRAORDINARY JUDY GARLAND IN A SPIRAL —

= LATE 30'S — MY OLDER BROTHER BEGINS HIS NON STOP REIGN OF TERROR — HIS CONSTANT RIDICULE — CAIN + ABEL — I SAID MY PRAYERS EVERY NIGHT — THEY WERE NEVER ANSWERED —

- MORE 30's — WHY DIDN'T I TELL MY PARENTS — WHY DID I THINK THAT GOD WOULD HELP ME — WHY COULDN'T I CRY —

- MY MOTHER — EVERY AFTERNOON WHILE WE WERE AT SCHOOL — THE HOUSE QUIET — MY MOTHER PLAYED THE PIANO — AT NIGHT AFTER A COUPLE OF DRINKS MY PARENTS WOULD DANCE FOR US — THE MUSIC — DIXIELAND THE RADIO — SHE SAID MY FATHER WAS A STRONG LEAD — THEY WOULD FOX TROT & TWO STEP — DO THE CHARLESTON & BLACK BOTTOM — WHEN THEY HAD GUESTS MY MOTHER PLAYED — WE SAT ON THE STAIRS BECAUSE CHILDREN SHOULD BE SEEN & NOT HEARD — IF IRISH PEOPLE DRINK TOO MUCH ALL HELL BREAKS LOOSE —

- PARIS 60's
DAVID BAILEY — THE COCKNEY PHOTOGRAPHER — TOLD ME THE ONLY WAY TO DEAL WITH THE FRENCH WAS ALWAYS SPEAK ENGLISH — AT THE TIME DAVID

was married to Catherine Daneuve – David was copying Irving Penn prompting Avedon to say "Bailey is a Penn without the ink – Stephan Meisel has made a fortune copying Avedon – Meisel is an Avedon without the dick –

— Late 30's – I knew my older brother was violent and dagerous – who can you tell if your a child – would anyone believe – He was good looking and an athlete – For years befor he died he had become a helpless petulant child –

— Late 30's – When I was thirteen a neighbur gave me my first blow job – total ecstacy – When I went to confession, I didn't consider it a sin + remained silent – I never went to confession or communion again – starting a life of rebellion + hatred for liars + hypocrites –

– My sister Joan was called a tomboy – she was as good as me at climbing trees – learning how to run like the wind was how we played – she defended me against my older brother – we were conspirators – she is a grandmother and super business woman – like me she's outspoken & passionate – she upsets the hell out of people – stupid people tax one's patience –

– London 60's – Cecil Beaton was a trip – such a fine photographer – when I met him at Vogue he called me "Dear Boy" – the editor at Vogue – determined to live in the past & terrified of the young cockney photographers – she was convinced sex did not belong in a fashion magazine – poor darling – she had all the warmth of Margaret Thatcher – out of ignorance she killed a lot of superb street photographs –

- MY BABY BROTHER PETER IS BRILLIANT — I MISS TALKING TO HIM — HE HAS THREE DEGREES FROM CHICAGO UNIVERSITY — WAS A STOCK BROKER LIVING IN THE HUDSON RIVER VALLEY — HE IS LOST — MY SISTER & I DON'T KNOW WHERE HE IS — HE HAD EGO PROBLEMS WITH MY FATHER THAT HURT HIM DEEPLY — AFTER WORLD WAR TWO AMERICA FELL APART — GOOD TASTE — GOOD MANNERS — LOST FOREVER — GREED — CORRUPTION — DECAY RULE MY AMERICA —

- 60's NEW YORK — PARIS — LONDON — DONNA MITCHEL WAS NOT MY FAVORITE PERSON — SHE WAS MY FAVORITE MODEL — SHE WAS SHORT FOR A MODEL & HAD BEAUTIFUL BREASTS — SHE WAS FROM THE BRONX — SHE WAS THE BEST MODEL OF THE 60's — THE GLAMAZONS (SHRIMPTON) GOT THE PUBLICITY — DONNA GOT THE PHOTOGRAPHERS. SHE COULD ACT — SHE HAD A PROBLEM WITH SPEED — HER HANDS WERE ICE COLD — THE FASHION EDITORS hated her because she was the future & they clung to the past — they still do — her pal was Antonio Lopez — a sensational illustrator — he died from AIDS alone & broke — the editors deserted him — he gave me a drawing of ~~Madonna~~ Donna in a bikini astride a Harley Davidson — Donna grew up watching Bette Davis in the dark. She's an actress now — we were never friends —

— mid 30's

My father taught us all how to swim in the cold-grey Atlantic Ocean — he would put me on his back & ~~swim~~ swim out past the breakers — as long as I with him I was fearless — Summer at the beach — clean white sand — sea grass on the dunes — hurricane fences — my mother under a beach umbrella — afraid of the sun — after sundown she would swim — trekking picnic lunch across dunes — bonfires at night — stars seem really close —

- 2003 - SEXUAL DESIRE TORMENTS US EVERY DAY - ORGANISED RELIGIONS INSULT OUR INTELLIGENCE - IT TOOK ME YEARS TO FORGET WHAT THE CHURCH TAUGHT - PEOPLE BELIEVE IN THE MYTH OF "IMMACULATE CONCEPTION" - AN EGG WITHOUT SPERM TO FERTILIZE IT - WHEN THAT STORY WAS WRITTEN PEOPLE BELIEVED THE EARTH WAS FLAT.

- IS THERE ANY DIFFERENCE BETWEEN A DRUG-MAKER AND A DRUG-DEALER.

- MID 30's -
WE PLAYED COWBOYS & INDIANS WHEN I WAS A KID - EVERYONE WANTED "SIX SHOOTERS" CHAPS - COWBOY HAT - I DREAMED ABOUT BEING AN INDIAN - I LEARNED TO RIDE BAREBACK - THE TRIBES SEEMED BEAUTIFUL - THEY TAUGHT THE LAND SACRED - THERE ARE SAVAGES & COWBOYS - WHICH ONE ARE YOU ??

— 2003 — STIGMA HAPPENS TO PEOPLE BORN NEGRO — JEW — HOMOSEXUAL. THE STIGMA ON PEOPLE BORN INSANE IS TRAGIC — YOUR FAMILY ABANDONS YOU BECAUSE OF SHAME — SOCIETY ABANDONS YOU OUT OF FEAR & GUILT — THE INSANE WERE CHAINED TO WALLS — BEDLAM MEANT A LIFE SENTENCE OF SUFFERING — THE PHARMACEUTICAL COMPANIES CREATED DRUGS THAT IMMOBILISED A VICTIM BOTH MENTALLY & PHYSICALLY — THESE DRUGS HAVE HORRENDOUS SIDE EFFECTS — DOCTORS PERSCRIBE DRUGS THEY HAVE NEVER TAKEN — THE MEDICAL & PHARMACEUTICAL INDUSTRIES HAVE GROWN RICH BECAUSE OF THE INSANE — PERHAPS LASERS WILL BE USED SOMEDAY — IN THE MEANTIME THERE IS AN ARMY OF MENTALLY ILL HUMAN BEINGS LEFT TO THE STREET — THE LUCKY WALK BY & LOOK THE OTHER WAY — "MAN'S INHUMANITY TO MAN" PERSISTS —

— EARLY 60'S — SUE HOFFMAN WAS MY SECRETARY — WHEN BREAKING UP WITH MY PAL LOUIS FAURER SHE DESTROYED ALL HIS CAMERAS — LOUIE WAS A GENIUS — HE WAS TREATED WITH L.S.D. ALONG WITH CAREY GRANT — SUE BECAME "SUPERSTAR" VIVA — ANDY WARHOL'S FIRST VICTIM — ANYONE WHO WENT NEAR ANDY BECAME A VICTIM — ANDY'S ASSISTANT GERALD MALANGA USED TO SEND ME STRANGE LETTERS WHICH MY WIFE DESTROYED — ANDY WAS EVERYWHERE + NOWHERE — ALWAYS OUTSIDE THE "IN CROWD" —

— 30'S GOOD MANNERS ARE ONE SIGN OF A CIVILIZED MAN — WE WERE TAUGHT CONSTANTLY — MY FATHER TOLD HIS THREE SONS THAT ALL WOMEN WERE TO BE TREATED WITH RESPECT — HIS PHILOSOPHY WAS THAT WOMEN + CHILDREN NEEDED A MAN'S PROTECTION — NOT BECAUSE THEY WERE WEAK — BUT BECAUSE WE WERE STRONGER —

— LATE 60'S NEW YORK —
JULES BUCK - A HOLLYWOOD PRODUCER + FORMER PHOTOGRAPHER SAW A 30 MINUTE UNDERGROUND FILM I PLANNED + DIRECTED — HE SENT ME TO WILLIAM MORRIS AGENCY TO SEE A YOUNG AGENT — THIS GUY WANTED ME TO WRITE AN OUTLINE FOR A FEATURE ON WHAT HE CALLED THE "SWINGING 60'S" — THIS SAME AGENT WANTED BERT STERN TO OUTLINE A STORY ABOUT HIS LONG TIME AFFAIR WITH MARYLIN MONROE — NEITHER ONE OF US WAS IN GOOD SHAPE — BURT HAD BEEN TURNED ON TO SPEED BY DOCTOR BISHOP — AT THE TIME THIS IDIOT WAS SHOOTING UP ALL OF CAST OF "HAIR" WHICH WAS ON BROADWAY — DR. BISHOP ALSO TURNED ON A FRIEND - MICHEL J. POLLARD WHO HAD A LEAD IN "BONNIE + CLYDE" — DR. FEELGOOD + BISHOP WERE LATER DISBARRED — TOO LATE TO SAVE A LOT OF PEOPLE — MR. BUCK INVITED ME TO A PARTY AT THE 21 CLUB —

PRODUCERS SAM SPIEGEL & DARYL ZANUCK WERE TO TOAST PETER O'TOOLE'S LATEST FILM — I WAS AT A TABLE WITH JOAN BUCK — LAUREN BACALL — ANDY WARHOL & MARISSA BERENSON — I LIKE MARISSA —

— SOME SCHITZOPHRENICS ARE VIOLENT — MY VIOLENCE WAS DIRECTED AT ME —

— 2003 — JACK KEROUACK SAID "FAME IS AN OLD NEWSPAPER BLOWING DOWN BLEEKER STREET" — HERE IN L.A. "CELEBRITIES" BECOME YESTERDAY'S NEWS QUICKLY — EVERY WHORE NEEDS A PIMP TO HUSTLE THEM — A PIMP IN GUCCI LOAFERS IS STILL A PIMP —

— 30'S HOUSE CALLS — SMALL TOWN — WHEN ONE OF US WAS ILL MY MOTHER TOOK OUR TEMPERATURE & THEN CALLED THE DOCTOR — HE WOULD COME AND EXAMINE US — THIS MAN WAS A COMFORT TO CHILDREN — I NEVER HEARD THE WORD MALPRACTICE — THERE WAS

A SMALL HOSPITAL IN THE NEXT TOWN — BECAUSE OF AN ACCIDENT ON MY BYCICLE I HAD A HERNIA OPERATION — LATER ON MY APPENDIX WERE REMOVED — I DO NOT RECALL BEING CIRCUMSIZED BUT REMEMBER HAVING MY TONSILS REMOVED — MY EARLY TRUST IN DOCTORS WAS SHATTERED LATER ON — LITTLE BOYS WERE NOT SUPPOSED TO CRY & I NEVER DID —

— 2000 — HOW I LOVE YOUNG PEOPLE — THEY EMBRACE TECHNOLOGY AND ARE SO PATIENT TEACHING ME — I LEARN SO MUCH FROM THEM — THEY MAKE ME RECALL AN OLD SONG LYRIC — "FOOLS RUSH IN WHERE ANGELS FEAR TO TREAD" — I DON'T TRUST ANGELS — IN L.A. THEY ARE THE MOTHS & I AM THE FLAME — BEING FAMOUS IN AMERICA IS EASY — GOING BEYOND FAME IS THE ONLY CHALLENGE — YOU NEED BRASS BALLS — A "LONER" IS SOMEONE WHO IS BORED BY OR AFRAID OF SOCIETY — A RECLUSE DOESN'T GIVE A DAMN —

— 30'S — IN MY TOWN THERE WAS A SMALL COUNTRY CLUB — IT WAS RESTRICTED-LIKE THE HAMPTONS — NO JEWS ALLOWED — AT THE BEACH THERE WAS A BEACH CLUB CALLED "LIDO" — IT WAS PRIVATE & ~~ALL~~ JEWISH — THE BEACHES — FROM CONEY ISLAND TO AMAGANSET — WERE CLEAN AND BEAUTIFUL — WHEN WE WERE KIDS WE WERE TAKEN TO CONEY ISLAND — IT WAS AN EARLY DISNEYLAND — WE HAD LUNA PARK — STEEPLECHASE — NATHAN'S SUPERB HOT DOGS — PEOPLE "DRESSED" TO GO — I HAVE TAKEN SO MANY PHOTOGRAPHS AT CONEY ISLAND — IT BECAME DERELICT AFTER THE WAR — ~~IT~~ BECOMING DANGEROUS & GANG INFESTED — THE GYPSIES & THEN THE PUERTO RICANS TOOK OVER — THE VERY SAME SQUALOR TOOK OVER ATLANTIC CITY & THE JERSEY SHORE — THE HAMPTONS WILL FOLLOW — THERE GOES THE NEIGHBORHOOD — THERE GOES THE COUNTRY —

→ 70's — As a six year old I was quite sure that I was grown — One night I informed my parents I was leaving — They packed a small suitcase & put me on the back porch — It was cold & dark & scarey — Deciding to leave some other time I rang the bell —

→ 2003 — I'm going to make a cup of coffee — have another Newport — and watch the news — another war — another pathetic award show for Hollywood — once again more exalted mediocrity — more vulgarity — Hollywood is being "gentrified" — they will have to fumigate it first — Think I'll walk my dog "Mick" — A Mick is a low class Irish designation — How appropo —

← Writing this is like going to confession — I have already done my penance —

– 2003 – WHEN PEOPLE SAY "YOU ARE NOT ALONE" – THAT'S ANOTHER LIE – YOU ARE LOCKED INSIDE YOUR OWN HEAD – YOU ARE ALONE – & YOU HAVE TO SAVE YOURSELF – YOU HAVE TO USE EGO & COURAGE TO IGNORE THAT KIND OF WELL MEANING LIE –

– 30'S LATE
SATURDAY MATINÉE – IF IT RAINED OR SNOWED ON A SATURDAY WE WERE ALLOWED TO GO TO THE MOVIES – THE SMALL ART DECO THEATER WAS NAMED THE "FANTASY" – ALL FILMS WERE STILL IN GLORIOUS BLACK & WHITE – THERE WAS THE "A" FEATURE & THE "B" CO-FEATURE – A SHORT FLASH GORDON OR BUCK RODGERS – AND A "NEWS OF THE WORLD" – WE COULD TAKE A BUS DOWN TO MAIN STREET – I REMEMBER IT ALL COSTING FIFTY CENTS – THERE WAS THE ORCHESTRA – THE LOGE FOR SMOKING & A BALCONY FOR TEENAGE "NECKING" –

– 30'S – BECAUSE I WAS TALL I SAT IN THE BACK ROW AT SCHOOL – EVERY MORNING WE HAD TO RECITE FROM MEMORY THE PREVIOUS NIGHTS HOMEWORK – WHEN WE FINISHED OUR HOMEWORK ONE OF MY PARENTS WOULD GO OVER IT – NO EXCUSE WAS ACCEPTED BY THE SISTERS – IF YOU FAILED YOUR FINAL EXAMS YOU HAD TO ATTEND SUMMER SCHOOL OR BE LEFT BACK & REPEAT AN ENTIRE YEAR – WE WENT TO THE BEACH EVERY DAY – AFTER SUPPER WE PLAYED "HIDE & SEEK" & "RING-A-LEEVEO" TILL DARK – I STILL LOVE STICK BALL – IF YOU HAD A GLASS JAR & METAL LID YOU COULD CAPTURE LIGHTENING BUGS – I WAS BORN AN INNOCENT CHILD – AND I SHALL DIE AN INNOCENT OLD MAN –

– 2003 – I LIVE ON TOP OF A MOUNTAIN IN A SMALL 1920'S BUNGALOW WITH SLIDING GLASS walls + a large front porch — very old trees + flowers everywhere — my dog "Mick" wakes me everyday at 6 AM. The sun rises and I let him run up on the road — at night the cyotes come up under my bedroom window — they prey on cats — I ~~cannot~~ can't imagine life without animals — life without music — life without beauty — + most of all life without children — In the distance I see the San Gabriel mountains topped with snow — below me — palm trees — Mexicans are everywhere in L.A. — some of them are actually legal — I have videotaped the gang bangers + also the cemetery where so many are buried — one night my windshields were shot out in a "drive by" — my car is a silver 1979 Mercedes — In the valley below me you can buy any drug you favor —

- 1960's – WHEN WE LIVED IN PARIS MY WIFE WHO IS JEWISH SAID THE FRENCH ARE WORSE THAN THE JEWS WITH THEIR PASSION FOR EVERY CENTIME. I THOUGHT THE ONLY THING THEY ADORED WAS LUNCH + DINNER –

- 2003 – PHOTOGRAPHING FASHION IN "WINDOWS" – THE RESTERAUNT ON THE TOP OF ONE OF THE TOWERS OF THE WORLD TRADE CENTER WAS AMAZING – YOU COULD SEE LONG ISLAND – NEW JERSEY – CONNECTICUT. THE HUDSON + EAST RIVERS OUT TO THE ATLANTIC OCEAN – I LOVE MY COUNTRY + MY ATTITUDE TOWARD TERRORISTS IS – "GO FUCK YOURSELF"

- 30's – I HAD A PAPER ROUTE IN THE ~~EIGHTH~~ SEVENTH GRADE MAKING SOME EXTRA MONEY TO AUGMENT MY SMALL WEEKLY ALLOWANCE – I COULD BUY DRAWING PADS + WATER COLORS –

One customer on my route was a lonely housewife who was sloshed every day — she would invite me in and talk non stop — all the time boozing — I think she was horney — but I was too young to know — her house smelled of wiskey + perfume — I never told anyone about her — I really like women who smell good — my father always said that a man when drunk was rediculous — a woman was pathetic —

— 30's — Leaving St. Agnes after eight years — my brother who was two years ahead of me — went to public high school — the next four years were the best he would have — star athlete — dating a cheerleader — he was a "jock" + a "stud" + a piss poor student — never cracked a book — why bother when your a "Greek God" —

— 1990's — My son Terry was photographing for "W" magazine. He had an exhibit in a Soho gallery of wonderful portraits of punk rock girls taken in East Village bars — one of the girls had a swastika on her knickers — the punks + the skinheads loved Nazi symbols — The "Ladies" at "W" dropped him + called him an anti-semite once again showing their ignorance + disregarding the fact that Terry is half Jewish — How do these broads get their jobs —

— 2003 — The only way America could be destroyed is to allow Americans to destroy it — Greed — Corruption — ~~Greed~~ decay running amock on every level of society — no country is perfect — one has to fight for freedom — If you don't fight then you deserve to lose it — The Irish say — It is

BETTER TO DIE ON YOUR FEET THAN TO LIVE ON YOUR KNEES" — MY YOUNG FRIENDS TELL ME THAT IN THIS COUNTRY MEN ACT LIKE WOMEN + WOMEN ACT LIKE MEN — NOT EVERY REVOLUTION ENDS WELL —

— 30'S — A NEIGHBOR WITH ADJOINING PROPERTY — SEPARATED BY A TALL HEDGE — CAUGHT MY SYMPATHY — WE WERE THE SAME AGE AND BOTH OUTSIDERS — SHE DIDN'T FIT IN EITHER — HER NAME WAS BARBARA — HER NAME IS A TATOO ON MY LEFT ARM — TWO LONELY CHILDREN SEPARATED BY A TALL HEDGE — HER FATHER WAS AN ENGINEER WHOSE WEALTH CAME FROM INVESTMENTS — MY PARENTS WERE NOT FOND OF THEM — SHE WOULD BECOME A CLEVER ALCOHOLIC — WHEN I STARTED FINDING EMPTY VODKA BOTTLES UNDER THE BED WE WERE NEWLY MARRIED — SHE FAVORED BOOZE AND BARBITURATES —

- 2003 — There is an updraft from the valley below me + the hawks glide by — their wing span is large + they can cruise by looking for prey — they are free and they are cruel — Most of the people on my mountain work in the film buisness — writers — agents — lawyers — they are not free — you can't fly with only your left wing mind set —

- 30's — My mother was a good cook — my favorite meal was Sunday roast — we had a large ice box that was fitted every few days with huge blocks of ice — the iceman + his tongs was ~~replaced~~ replaced by a fridge — we had ice box cake — angelfood + upside down apricot cake — pies had to cool on the kitchen window sill — In the summer my mother made strawberry preserves in glass jars topped with parafin wax —

1960-2003 - HARPER'S BAZAAR IN THE SIXTIES WAS STILL THE ONLY GREAT FASHION JOURNAL ON THE PLANET - THE BAZAAR THAT IS PUBLISHED TODAY IS THE WORST - MEDIOCRITY AND VULGARITY RULE - EDITORS ARE HIRED AND FIRED - CREATIVE DIRECTORS STEAL IDEAS FROM THE ARCHIVES - LIKE EVERYONE IN THE FASHION INDUSTRY - THEY LOOK TO THE PAST FOR IDEAS - THEY CAN NOT FORECAST THE FUTURE - NOSTALGIA KILLS CREATIVITY - MRS. VREELAND TOLD US TO DO WHAT WE WANTED BUT THE PHOTOGRAPHS HAD TO BE "DEVINE" - HER FAVORITE WORD - TODAY ALL THE PHOTOGRAPHY LOOKS AS THOUGH ONE PERSON IS DOING IT ALL - PHOTOGRAPHERS PLAY A GAME CALLED "GRAB THE MONEY AND RUN" - THAT'S THE SAME GAME PROSTITUTES HAVE ALWAYS FAVORED - FROM DICK AVEDON TO STEVEN MEISEL IS A TRIP FROM THE PENTHOUSE TO THE BASEMENT -

- 2003 – WHY IS IT TAKING SO LONG FOR ROCK + ROLL TO DIE – IN L.A. THERE ARE THOUSANDS OF BANDS MAKING NOISE – BLACK – WHITE – LATINO – MUSIC VIDEOS ARE ~~PREVIOUS~~ ~~AND~~ NUMBING – IN THE 50'S COOL JAZZ AND BEBOP LANGUISHED + ROCK EXPLODED – WHAT WILL THE NEXT EXPLOSION SOUND LIKE – WILL ANYONE BE ABLE TO HEAR IT –

- 60'S – ~~HENRY WOLF~~ THERE HAVE BEEN THREE INNOVATIVE ART DIRECTORS IN THE MAGAZINE WORLD – ALEXI BRODOVITCH – ~~HENRY~~ HENRY WOLF – MARVIN ISRAEL – AFTER THEM ONLY GUTLESS IMITATORS – ~~BIG~~ HENRY ~~WOLF~~ REPLACED MR. BRODOVITCH AT BAZAAR – HE DISCOVERED MELVIN SOKOLSKY WHOSE WORK IS STILL BEING COPIED – AT THE TIME HENRY WAS LIVING WITH ALI McGRAW WHO ASSISTED MELVIN – I PHOTOGRAPHED SOME

Advertising ~~campaigns~~ CAMPAINS for Henry — he would give me one of his strange ideas & I would interpret them for him — his layouts were beautiful — he's a photographe now — Ali McGraw became a film actress (we worked together in Marvin Israel's studio — it was an old water tower — Marvin told Ali she had too much money — being Mrs. Bob Evans irritated feisty Marvin — I photographed Marvin as a mad scientist for Henry — Marvin was crazy like a fox — a cornered fox — at a dinner party Fabien Baron sat across from Henry — every photographer knows that Fabien (then at Bazaar) was ripping off Henry's brilliant original ideas — Fabien did Madonna's Sex book with Steven Meisel — it was not well received — what would some people do without obnoxious publicists pimping for them —

— 2003 — MY WONDERFUL SON WAS RECENTLY TREATED FOR HEROIN ADDICTION — I WOULD LOVE TO HAVE FIVE MINUTES ALONE WITH THE PERSON WHO WAS SUPPLYING HIM — HE IS STRAIGHT NOW + WILL BE DOING HIS FIRST FILM — I WOULD LIKE TO LIVE LONG ENOUGH TO SEE IT — I WANT TO BE A GRANDFATHER — I WASN'T ABLE TO BE GOOD FATHER — WHAT A GOOD GRANDFATHER BOB RICHARDSON COULD BE — WHEN TERRY WAS YOUNG I TAUGHT HIM TO WALK — TO SWIM — IN NEW YORK — PARIS — TANGIER — ATHENS — LONDON — I HAVE LEARNED UNCONDITIONAL LOVE BECAUSE OF HIM — THE TRICK IS TO LISTEN — TO FORGET EGO — TO BUILD HIS — IT'S GREAT TO HAVE A SON WHOSE PHOTOGRAPHS WOW ME — I TEACH HIM TO USE ALL OF HIS SUFFERING IN HIS WORK THE WAY ALL ARTISTS HAVE — TERRY IS MY REVENGE —

- '30's – One day my older brother brought a friend of his down to my corner of the cellar – working on a landscape – trying to get the color right – he pointed to it & laughed – the sneer & contempt & hatred is a memory that hurts no longer because I am writing about it – Some of my best photographs have been landscapes – thank God for the camera – it will record a landscape in a fraction of a second – thank God for my brother –

- 30's – When my parents fought they would go upstairs to their bedroom – close the door and have it out –

- 2003 – Recently around midnight while walking my dog – a guy came at me out of the dark – I saw him raise his hand — my dog lunged & bit him — the guy screamed & took off — I got down on my knees & had a talk with this pal of mine — when I adopted him at the pound he had one more day to live — he hustles me for dog biscuits — when I take him to parties or openings he never leaves my side — he's a mutt —

— 2003 — there are two kinds of photographers — the genius & the mediocre — which one are you —

— 2003 — plastic surgery leaves a woman with an old face sans lines & wrinkles — nothing can change hungry-tired eyes — to have a face like a mask on top of a sagging body is grotesque — plastic boobs do not make a woman sexual — they makes a woman a willing victim —

— 40's — Found out that my older brother and his friend from Junior Varsity Football Team were going each afternoon to a boys house where this kid would give each one a blow job — If you have any kind of sex with another male can you still brag about being straight?

2003
— All photographers hate photography critics because they see things in an artist's work that are not there — The critic reveals more about himself than the photographer he's profiling — Why doesn't the critic just say "I like these pictures — perhaps you will too" — Maybe the problem stems from the fact they are paid by the word.

— 2003 — Saw a photo this A.M. in the L.A. Times of an actress I lived with in the 70's — she still looks beautiful —

- 2003 – Humphrey Bogart & Bette Davis spent their lives entertaining us in the dark – they never told us how to vote or what to think –

- 2003 – Saw the Stones in concert on T.V. last night – half Geritol – half acid – the music sounded better forty years ago when it was half Jack Daniels – half acid –

- 30's – It's funny + sad when a kid is naked in a locker room full of other kids – + everyone is pretending not to look –

- 30's – Spent many afternoon looking at the family photo album – wonderful photographs taken by Box Brownie camera – lovely quality – photos at the beach – with the family buick – at the Delaware Water Gap – on the Boardwalk – in the 60's

I DUPLICATED THEM FROM MEMORY — I CAN RECALL THE SMALLEST DETAILS — THE CLOTHES — THE SHOES — THE SIMPLICITY OF THE FRAMING — THE CHOICE OF BACKGROUNDS — ALL IN BLACK & WHITE — COLOR ISN'T REAL — IT'S JUST VULGAR — WE ALL HAD BIG EARS — STRONG JAW LINES & CHEEK BONES —

= 30'S — CHILDREN ARE LIKE ANIMALS — IF YOU ARE CRUEL TO THEM LONG ENOUGH — THEY WILL TURN ON YOU — THE FACT THAT CHILDREN TAKE WEAPONS TO SCHOOL DOES NOT SURPRISE ME — SOME CHILDREN — BECAUSE OF THE WAY THEY LOOK OR BEHAVE — BECOME A TARGET — THEIR TORMENTORS TRAVEL IN PACKS — I NEVER TOLD MY PARENTS THAT I WAS A TARGET — THAT WOULD HAVE INCREASED THE HUMILIATION — WHERE DID ALL THIS PRIDE COME FROM — EIGHT YEARS OF HELL AT SAINT AGNES ACADEMY —

40's — ENTERING PUBLIC HIGH SCHOOL MEANT NO MORE NUNS + PRIESTS — NO MORE BENEDICTION AFTER SCHOOL — NO MORE DAILY CHATS ABOUT SAINTS WHO WERE HAPPY TO BE BURNED AT THE STAKE — ABSTINENCE MAKES YOU EXTREMELY HORNY — DIDN'T THE NUNS KNOW THAT — TELLING KIDS THEY WOULD BURN IN HELL IF THEY HAD SEX BEFORE MARRIAGE — SADISTS IN RELIGIOUS COSTUMES — PRAYING ON MY KNEES FOR EIGHT YEARS FOR GUIDANCE THAT NEVER CAME — I TURNED AGAINST THEIR GOD + BEGAN TRYING TO FIND MY OWN GOD — NEVER REALISING WHERE HE WAS — MY FATHER TOLD ME ONCE THAT FAITH IS BELEIVING IN WHAT YOU CAN NOT SEE OR UNDERSTAND — BEAUTY BECAME MY GOD — SEEING IS THE ONLY WAY TO BELIEVE — IN HIGH SCHOOL EVERYTING CHANGED — NO MORE LANDSCAPES — NO MORE FLOWERS — ENTER THE DESIGN PHASE —

— 40'S — DURING FOUR YEARS AT HIGH SCHOOL DESIGNING BECAME SOMETHING ALL CONSUMING — I MADE THOUSANDS OF LINE DRAWINGS OF CARS & AIRPLANES — BOTTLES & BOXES — CLOTHES & ACCESSORIES — WALLPAPER & FABRICS — I FOUND OUT LATER THERE WAS A BOY MY AGE IN A DIFFERENT PLACE DOING THE SAME THING — ANDY WARHOLA — POLISH NOT IRISH — BUT DRIVEN — THERE WAS MISS DENNISON — THE ART TEACHER — TALL & THIN WITH PIERCING BLUE EYES — LOOKING FOR YOUNG PEOPLE TO INSPIRE — GOD BLESS YOU MISS DENNISON — SHE HAD SOMETHING I'VE NEVER FORGOTTEN — HER OWN STYLE — THE FRENCH SAY THE WORD "CHIC" CANNOT BE DEFINED — YOU EITHER GOT IT OR YOU AIN'T — SHE HAD IT — SHE ALLWAYS SMELLED GOOD — FOR AN OLD LADY SHE HAD BEAUTIFUL LEGS — THERE WAS A GIRL IN ART CLASS WHOSE DRAWINGS WERE MORE SKILLFUL THAN MINE — WE WERE FRIENDS FOR FOUR YEARS —

→ 40's – THE WAR NEWS FROM EUROPE WAS IGNORED – IN THE 1930'S EUROPE WAS SO FAR AWAY – JUST LIKE TODAY THE IDIOTS SAID IT WASN'T OUR PROBLEM – THAT ALL CHANGED – WE HAD F.D.R. WHO WAS A STATESMAN TO LEAD US – NOW WE HAVE POLITICIANS WHO CAN'T LEAD A GIRL SCOUT TROOP – THEY ARE TOO BUSY RETURNING FAVORS & HOPEING TO BE RE-ELECTED THE WORLD ALSO HAD WINSTON CHURCHILL – MY FATHER'S HERO – WE WERE TAUGHT THAT THE JAPANESE WERE THE "YELLOW PERIL" THE ENGLISH LANGUAGE IS SO EXTRAORDINARY –

– 2003 – THE WHOLE IDEA OF DEMOCRACY – COMMUNISM – OR SOCIALISM IS IDEALISM AT IT'S MOST PATHETIC – ALL THREE "ISM'S" EXIST BUT NOT WITH ANY TRUTH – ALL THREE ARE GOOD IDEAS THAT WILL NEVER BE REALIZED – NOT ON THIS PLANET –

— 2003 — "REPORTAGE" IS WONDERFUL — IT IS SECOND NATURE TO ME WITH A CAMERA — BUT NEW AND DIFFICULT WITH WORDS — "A PHOTOGRAPH IS BETTER THAN A THOUSAND WORDS" IS MORE BULL SHIT — THE RIGHT WORD CAN GIVE YOU A THOUSAND IMAGES —

— 2003 — RECENTLY AN L.A. "CELEBRITY" PHOTOGRAPHER DIED FROM A.I.D.S. — HE WAS 50 YEARS OLD + RICH — I AM 75 YEARS OLD + ALWAYS BROKE — WOULD I CHANGE PLACES — HELL NO — WOULD HE CHANGE PLACES — HELL NO — DO YOUR BEST WITH THE CARDS YOU ARE DEALT —

— 2003 — THERE ARE SEXUAL ACTS THAT HAVE NOTHING TO DO WITH LOVE MAKING + EVERYTHING TO DO WITH SEXUAL HUNGER — THE NEED TO TASTE — TO SMELL — TO TOUCH — NATURE GAVE US A MOUTH + A TONGUE — WHEN WE ARE BORN WE SUCK ON SOMETHING FOR PLEASURE + NURISHMENT —

- 40'S – THE MUSIC WAS FOR DANCING THE LINDY – AND TO SLOW DANCE UP CLOSE – THE BANDS WERE BENNY GOODMAN – HARRY JAMES – WOODY HERMAN – GENE KRUPA – CLAUDE THORNHILL – TOMMY DORSEY – THE BAND SINGERS – FRANK SINATRA – PEGGY LEE – ANITA O'DAY – CHRIS O'CONNOR – SCHOOL DANCES IN THE GYMNASIUM – HEAVY PETTING – SMOKING LUCKIES & CAMELS – BOBBY SOX – TRYING ILLISIT MANHATTANS – BACK SEAT TRYSTS IN YOUR FATHER'S BUICK – GOING STEADY – THE LAST INNOCENT GENERATION WILL MISS WORLD WAR 2 BUT KOREA'S ON THE HORIZON –

- MISS SHERMAN WAS MY ENGLISH TEACHER WHILE A SOPHMORE – SHE KEPT ME AFTER SCHOOL & TOLD SHE KNEW I WAS LONELY – SHE GAVE ME A READING LIST – MUCH LATER I READ 2 OR 3 BOOKS A WEEK WHILE RECOVERING MY SANITY –

— 2003. JEAN COCTEAU SAID THAT STYLE IS A SIMPLE WAY TO SAY COMPLICATED THINGS — FASHION HAS NOTHING TO WITH STYLE OR CHIC — IT'S NOT THE CLOTHES — IT THE WAY YOU WEAR THEM — WHO HAS CHIC — MARLENE DIETRICH — GARBO — CHANEL — DIANA VREELAND — FRED ASTAIR — BOB DYLAN — MAUGHAM — KEITH RICHARDS — BETTY ~~BE CATTREW~~ CATTREAU — ANNA PIAGI — CASATI — BEATON — FRANK LLOYD WRIGHT — JOHN HOUSTON — VISCONTI — JOHN GALLIANO — IRIS BIANCI — CHINA MACHADO — ANITA PALENBERG — CHE GUEVERA — MICK JAGGER — OSCAR DE LA RENTA —

— 40'S — AN OLDER BOY WANTED TO HAVE SEX WITH ME — I TOLD HIM I WANTED HIM TO BE MY FRIEND — IN SENIOR HIGH THIS GUY WAS CAPTAIN OF THE FOOTBALL TEAM —

- 40's – FOR A LONG TIME I WAS PART OF A SMALL GROUP OF FRIENDS – I KNEW I DIDN'T BELONG – THEY TURNED ON ME AS A SENIOR BECAUSE I KEPT CHANGING – I WAS SO INTO GOING HOME AND DRAWING WITH INDIA INK AND BRUSH – HUNDREDS OF SIMPLE ~~GRAPHIC~~ LINE DRAWINGS – I LOVED DRAWING MONKEYS – DID HUNDREDS OF LINE DRAWINGS OF CLOSE UPS OF WOMEN AND MEN – THEY LOOKED LIKE FASHION DRAWINGS – I SIGNED ALL OF THEM – FAVORITE CLASSES – ENGLISH – HISTORY – WORST GRADES IN MATH OR SCIENCE – AND ART CLASS WAS HELD IN STUDIO UNDER LARGE SKYLIGHTS – I MANAGED TO LEARN SOME SPANISH – LOVE ALL THINGS SPANISH –

— 2003 - SITTING IN MY LIVING ROOM — LATE AFTERNOON — OUTSIDE MY WINDOWS THERE IS A STORM ~~CLOUDS~~ — BEAUTIFUL CLOUDS COMING — T.V. ~~IN~~ THE CORNER ON WITHOUT THE SOUND — WOULD LIKE TO LIVE AS LONG AS I CAN WORK — DIE TRYING TO DO SOMETHING PERFECT — RIGHT NOW I NEED TO KEEP GOING — TAKE CARE OF ME + MY DOG — LIKE TALKING FILM WITH TERRY — HE HAS A SECRET INNERLIFE — SO DO I —

— 40'S — THERE WAS A 30'S SODA FOUNTAIN IN THE VILLAGE — IF YOU WERE "POPULAR" YOU SPENT THE AFTERNOON THERE I WISH SOMETIMES THAT A LEMON COKE & A GRILLED CHEESE SANDWICH WOULD MAKE A COMEBACK — THE GIRLS SAT BY THEMSELVES + CHATTERED — THE BOYS SAT + ~~BO~~ BOASTED —

- 40'S – IN ORDER TO BE "POPULAR" YOU HAD TO BE STUPID AND INSENSITIVE OR A BRILLIANT ACTOR – FOR THREE YEARS I LED A DOUBLE LIFE – THE HUNGER FOR FRIENDSHIP AND ACCEPTANCE AT SCHOOL AND THE TIME AT HOME DRAWING AND DESIGNING – IN THE END MY OTHER "POPULAR" FRIENDS ABANDONED + SCORNED ME AS AN OUTSIDER – BEING AN OUTSIDER – A MAVERICK – A REBEL BECAME MY LIFE – YOU CAN NOT CHANGE WHO YOU ARE – THAT'S NOT IN THE CARDS –

- 2003 – LIVING WITH LONELINESS CAN BE PAINFUL – YESTERDAY WAS A STRUGGEL TO STAY "UP" – LAST NIGHT MY SON CALLED + I WASN'T LONELY ANYMORE – HE WAS WATCHING A BLIZZARD IN NEW YORK + WE TALKED FOR AN HOUR – WHEN I SAY GOODBYE IT'S DIFFICULT – HE TELL'S ME HE LOVES ME –

- 40's – LOST MY "CHERRY" AT 17 – KIDS LOSE IT NOW AT 12 – A FRIEND OF MINE HAD A GIRLFRIEND WHO LIKED "GANG BANGS" – WHEN IT WAS MY TURN IT WAS FAST + FURIOUS –

- 2003 – PERHAPS MY GENERATION OF ARTISTS HAD TO LEAVE SOMETHING TO THE IMAGINATION – CENSORSHIP FORCES YOU TO USE YOUR IMAGINATION – SOME OF THE BEST LITERATURE AND FILMS THIS COUNTRY HAS PRODUCED HAD TO PASS THE CENSORS – THIS WORK FORCED US TO USE OUR IMAGINATION – THAT NO LONGER EXISTS – EVERYTHING IS REVEALED – THERE IS NO ESCAPE –

- 40's – MY BROTHERS + SISTER WERE TALKING COLLEGE – HIGHER MATH + BUSINESS ADMINISTRATION – MY DREAM WAS ART SCHOOL –

— 40's — Millions of Americans believed that Hitler was not a threat — he was so far away — cowards allways say that death & destruction is someone else's problem — and then it's too late — every country has an army & and a police force to fight & die so that the cowards can dream. Which one are you — while in high school I heard about concentration camps at home — never in school — "Don't upset the children" is an excuse for avoiding hideous realities —

— 2003 — Dreaming often about a woman who left me makes me smile — in these dreams she is always young — now at middle age she is still beautiful — she left me for a man who eventually left her — I did not tell her that I was schizophrenic. —

– 40's – AND THEN THERE WAS PEARL HARBOR – WE WERE TAUGHT THAT THE "JAPS" WERE THE "YELLOW PERIL" – MY OLDER BROTHER HAVING FINISHED HIGH SCHOOL ENLISTED IN THE NAVY – WAS IT BECAUSE HE LOVED THE SEA OR BECAUSE HE LOVED THE SKIN TIGHT UNIFORM. MY FATHER WAS PROUD OF HIM – HAVING A BEDROOM TO MYSELF WAS LOVELY – IF YOU STUDY HISTORY YOU REALIZE THAT ATI WAR MOVIES ARE A WASTE OF TIME – LOUIS B. MAYER SAID THAT IF YOU WANT TO SEND A MESSAGE – USE WESTERN UNION – YOUNG PEOPLE SHOULD GO TO SCHOOL FOR AN EDUCATION & GO TO A MOVIE TO BE ENTERTAINED –

– 40's – FRANK SINATRA HAD ALL OF THESE YOUNG GIRLS SCREAMING & SWOONING – WHEN ASKED IF BEING COPIED BOTHERED HIM – HE SAID "THEY HAVE ALL THE TECHNIQUE & NONE OF THE MISTICQUE"

– 40's – WINSTON CHURCHILL TOLD THE GERMANS TO FUCK OFF – SOMEONE WHO CAN KNOCK BACK A BOTTLE OF BRANDY EVERY DAY & STILL HAVE THE CHUTSPA TO TURN THE TABLES ON THE "SUPERMEN" IS A GENIUS – HE SAID THE GERMANS ARE AT YOUR THROAT OR AT YOUR FEET – LATER ON HE SPENT HIS TIME PAINTING LANDSCAPES –

– 40's – BRIDGE WAS A GAME MY PARENTS ADORED – THERE WAS RITUAL INVOLVED – THE BEAUTIFUL CARD TABLE & CHAIRS – THE CIGARETS & MARTINIS – THE QUIET CONCENTRATION – PLAYING WITH A PARTNER FOR "DOUBLES"

– 2003 – WHY CAN'T LIFE BE MORE THAN CHANCE – WHY CAN'T THERE BE A GOD GUIDING US – WHERE DID THE WORD GOD COME FROM – WHY DOES THE WORLD CRAVE AN AFTERLIFE –

- 40'S – JUNIOR YEAR – THE CUTEST GIRL AND A CHEERLEADER FASCINATED ME – SHORT GIRLS APPEALED TO ME BECAUSE IT WAS EASY TO HOLD THEM – LATER ON THEY HAD TO BE TALL –

- 40'S – SATURDAY AFTERNOONS IN COLD WEATHER WERE FOOTBALL – LATER ON FRIDAY NIGHTS WERE BASKETBALL IN THE GYMNASIUM – MY OLDER BROTHER WAS A "NATURAL" IN HIGH SCHOOL + COLLEGE – THERE WERE NO MORE CHEERS FOR HIM AFTER EIGHT GLORIOUS YEARS – MY YOUNGER BROTHER + I DID NOT CHOOSE TO BE COMPARED –

- 40'S – STARTED DOING DRAWINGS OF WOMEN – THEY LOOKED LIKE FASHION DRAWINGS – THE BEST DRAWINGS WERE DONE WITHOUT A MODEL – STARTED TAKING LONG ISLAND RAILROAD ONE NIGHT A WEEK FOR "LIFE CLASSES" AT

THE ART STUDENT'S LEAGUE ON 57 ST. — DRAWING NUDE MODELS MOST OF WHOM WERE DANCERS — WENT TO THE AUTOMAT NEAR CARNEGIE HALL FOR COFFEE — TO BE IN A CLASS FULL OF PEOPLE LIKE ME WAS MY INTRODUCTION — MY PASSPORT — TO A LIFE I DREAMED ABOUT — TEARING DOWN PENN STATION WAS ANOTHER MISTAK GOING TO GET A TRAIN HOME WITH MY DRAWING PADS WAS THE FIRST TIME I FELT GROWN UP — WHAT A SOPHISTICATED BOY I WAS — STARTING THEN THE CLASSMATES I SO WANTED TO BE A PART OF SEEMED LIKE ENEMIES I WAS GOING TO ESCAPE — ESCAPING THE TOWN AND MY FAMILY WAS A GOAL — HOW STRANGE TO LOVE PEOPLE WHO WERE SO UNLIKE YOURSELF — BEING THE BLACK SHEEP IN A FAMILY HURTS — BECOMING A "HOLY TERROR" IS THE ONLY WAY OUT — IT NEVER OCCURED TO ME TO SHOW MY DRAWINGS TO ANYONE —

– 40'S – WHEN WE TURNED SIXTEEN WE WERE ALLOWED TO SMOKE IN THE HOUSE + TO DRIVE – MY FATHER TAUGHT EACH ONE OF US TO DRIVE – LECTURING US ABOUT SAFETY – YEARS LATER HE WAS DRIVING WHEN MY MOTHER WAS KILLED – LIKE MY PARENTS I HAVE SMOKED FOR SIXTY YEARS – IS IT DANGEROUS – YES – SO IS DRIVING AN L.A. FREEWAY – I THINK STUPIDITY + APATHY KILL MORE AMERICANS THAN CIGARETTES + GUNS –

– 2003 – MOVIE "STARS" ARE PAID MILLIONS OF DOLLARS TO MAKE COMIC BOOK MOVIES – THEY SEND THEIR CHILDREN TO SCHOOL WHERE THEIR TEACHERS WOULD HAVE TO WORK TWO LIFETIMES TO MAKE WHAT THESE PEOPLE EARN FOR A FEW MONTH'S WORK – "HOORAY FOR HOLLYWOOD" –

- 2003 – YOU CAN BELONG TO THE HERD WHERE THERE IS SAFETY IN LOCKSTEP – OR YOU CAN BE AN INDEPENDENT – WILD & FREE & ALWAYS IN DANGER – WHICH ONE ARE YOU –

- ~~2003~~ 2003 – LOS FELIZ HAS A CAFÉ THAT I STOP BY – COFFEE IS CIVILISED – AT EVERY TABLE – ARMED WITH A LAPTOP & CELL PHONE – YOU FIND YOUNG PEOPLE FURIOUSLY KNOCKING OUT THE GREAT AMERICAN SCREENPLAY – WRITING IS USUALLY A LONELY PURSUIT – BUT NOT WITH A GENERATION BLASTED WITH IMAGES & SOUND – PERHAPS THEY ARE RIGHT –

- 2003 – WHEN INTERVIEWED ON FRENCH TELEVISION BEFORE HER DEATH – CHANEL SAID THAT AMERICAN FASHION EDITORS WERE "COWS" – WILL KARL LAGERFELD

MAKE MORE MONEY BEHIND THE GENIUS OF CHANEL THAN CHANEL MADE =

→ 40'S — HIGH SCHOOL BECAME ONE MORE ENDURANCE TEST — WE LIVED CLOSE TO THE BEACH + ON VACATIONS, I WOULD HITCH HIKE EVERY MORNING TO THE ATLANTIC — IF YOU COULD SWIM IN THIS DARK GREY SEA — YOU COULD SWIM ANYWHERE — YOUNG PEOPLE WOULD HITCH HIKE ACROSS THE COUNTRY — NO MORE — MEN CALLED HOBOS RODE THE RAILS — AMERICANS ARE ALWAYS RESTLESS —

→ 40'S — IN EUROPE THE GERMANS WERE GIVING THE WORD "BARBARIC" A WHOLE NEW MEANING — FROM BAUHAUS TO NO HOUSE — MILLIONS OF RUSSIANS DYING DEFENDING THEIR HOMELAND — THE FRENCH COLABORATING + SURRENDERING — DESPITE THE NIGHTLY BUZZ BOMBS — ENGLAND STILL HAD THEIR FUCK YOU ATTITUDE — SO FAR AWAY —

— 40'S — MY FATHER VERY SUPPORTIVE ABOUT ART SCHOOL — PARSON'S SCHOOL OF DESIGN SOUNDED VERY SOPHISTICATED — TWO MORE YEARS OF WAITING — WE SEEM TO SPEND SO MUCH TIME WAITING — WALKING AROUND WITH AN ERECTION ALL DAY — SIZE COUNTS — BUT NOT IF YOU HAVE TO TRY TO HIDE IT — IN THE HIGH SCHOOL I ATTENDED ADOLESCENTS ARE NOW GIVEN CONDOMS AND SEX EDUCATION CLASSES — THERE WERE NO TEEN PREGNANCIES + NO ABORTIONS — JUST HEAVY PETTING AND "GOING STEADY" — ALL THAT INNOSENCE GONE — AFTER THE WAR FREUD ARRIVES.

— 40'S — IN A MOSTLY WORKING CLASS TOWN NEAR BY — THERE WAS A ROAD HOUSE WITH A GOOD JUKE BOX — ALL THE BOYS PRETENDING TO BE MEN — RYE WISKEY AND GINGER ALE — NO "CARDING" — PUKE IN THE PARKING LOT —

— 2003 — BEAUTIFUL WINTER DAY IN CALIFORNIA — TOOK MY DOG FOR A WALK AT SIX A.M. — ANSWERED THREE DAYS OF VOICE MAIL MESSAGES — A GOOD FRIEND CANCELS A DINNER INVITATION FOR THE SECOND TIME — SAW A JOHN GARFIELD & JOAN CRAWFORD MOVIE LAST NIGHT — BLACK & WHITE PHOTOGRAPHY WAS LUMINUS — BOTH ACTORS WERE YOUNG — SO MANY BEAUTIFUL CLOSE UPS ~~OF BOTH ACTORS~~ — MANY SCENES WITH HAUNTING MUSIC & LITTLE ~~DIOL~~ DIOLOUGE — BIG SHOULDERS ON HER — COSTUME DESIGNERS LIKE ADRIAN COULD INFLUENCE AMERICAN WOMEN WITH ONE FILM MORE THAN CALVIN KLINE & TOM FORD COMBINED FROM GENIUS TO "GARMENTO" —

— 40'S — THERE WAS NO DIVORCE — MARRIED COUPLES SOLDIERED ON — NO BROKEN SINGLE PARENT HOMES — NOT IN MY TOWN —

– 40's – "CIRCLE JERKS" VERY OFTEN LED TO "I'LL DO YOU IF YOU'LL DO ME" – AND I DID –

– 2003 – THE ONLY MAGAZINE EDITOR TO SEND ME A BEAUTIFUL NOTE THANKING ME FOR AN ASSIGNMENT CAME FROM JOHN KENNEDY – INTELLIGENCE AND BREEDING ARE NON EXISTANT IN AMERICAN FASHION MAGAZINES – WHAT YOU HAVE ARE EDITORS WHO "BROWN NOSE" ADVERTISERS –

– 2003 – JOHN GALLIANO IS TODAY'S "BÉBÉ" BERARD – HE SHOULD BE DOING BALLETS & THE CIRCUS – DIAGHILEV WOULD LOVE HIM – ALEXANDER MCQUEEN SHOULD DO VEGAS – ERTÉ WOULD LOVE HIM –

– 2003 – TODAY'S PHOTOGRAPHERS LACK GENIUS – ORIGINALITY – TEMPERMENT – THEY WANT MONEY THEY SPEND BADLY & FAME THEY CAN'T HOLD ONTO –

— 40'S — WHEN PARENTS DO BATTLE OVER A CHILD — IT IS THE CHILD WHO SUFFERS — MY YOUNGER BROTHER SUFFERED MORE THAN ME BECAUSE OF MY FATHER'S ADMIRATION FOR HIS FIRST BORN — THE "PRODIGAL SON" WAS HOW I WAS PERCEIVED AFTER YEARS OF NOT CALLING HOME — MY MOTHER CALLED THE POLICE ONCE AFTER MY KID BROTHER DECKED HER VERY DEMANDING HUSBAND — ARE VOLATILE TEMPERS GENETIC — MY SON ONLY USES HIS TEMPER TOWARD THOSE WHO ARE CLOSE TO HIM — HIS MOTHER CALLED THE POLICE TO STOP HIS RAGE — HE LEFT HOME AT AN EARLY AGE — AT THAT POINT HIS FATHER WAS HOMELESS — MY FAMILY WAS NOT DYSFUNCTIONAL — MY COUNTRY IS DYSFUNCTIONAL —

— 30'S — OUR SMALL TOWN DENTIST WAS A SADIST ACCORDING TO WHAT HIS SON TOLD ME — MY FATHER tried to have ~~him b~~ his license taken away after he worked on me without novacaine — this son of a bitch pinned me to the chair & called me a coward for screaming in pain — this produced a life long terror of dentists —

— 2003 — winter rains tend to shoot down L.A.'s reputation as a sunny paradise — today the sky over Pasadena is gunmetal & there's a strong updraft from the valley below — many "anti-war" signs in town but the movie "stars" still ~~have not~~ have not told America what to do or think — the real war seems to be between the left & the right — the truth is never considered — the peacenicks have never read world history — they are too busy causing traffic jams on Wilshire ~~Rd~~ the leaders are "B-list" actors famous for bad films —

— 40'S — WITH POOR GRADES IN HIGH SCHOOL DOGGING ME — DRAWING EVERY AFTERNOON TURNED TO ARCHITECTURE — GOING TO NEW YORK AND SEEING THE TALL BUILDINGS EXCITED ME — WHAT WILL I DO IN THE FUTURE — WHAT WILL HAPPEN AFTER ART SCHOOL — THERE WAS NEVER A CHANCE TO DO ANYTHING ONE ISN'T BORN TO DO — YOU DO NOT CHOOSE TO BE AN ARTIST — IT CLAIMS YOU — BECOMING A BEATNICK AWAITED —

— 40'S — EVERY YEAR THERE WAS AN "ALL MEN BROKE" DANCE HELD IN THE GYM — GIRLS COULD ASK THE BOYS & PAID FOR THE TICKETS — THE GYM TEACHERS WERE THE CHAPERONES — WOMEN NOW CALL MEN TO ASK THEM FOR A DATE & ARE EXPECTED TO PAY HALF OF THE TAB — MEN NO LONGER HOLD A DOOR OPEN FOR A "LADY" — THE REVOLUTION HAS A DOWN SIDE —

– 2003 – THERE ARE WOMEN ON THE FASHION MAGAZINES WHO SPEND MOST OF THEIR TIME HANGING OUT WITH GAY MEN – THEY BEAR THE SOBRIQUET "FAG HAG" – POOR DARLINGS –

– 40's – HIGH SCHOOL GRADUATION IS LOOMING – THEN WHAT – STARTING TO THINK ABOUT ESCAPE – HAVE DREAMS OF LIVING IN GREENWICH VILLAGE – BEAUTIFUL OLD HOUSES & IT'S OWN HISTORY – IT WOULD TAKE TIME TO FLEE – BEING AN OUTCAST IS PAINFUL –

– 2003 – THERE'S A FAMOUS PHOTOGRAPHER WHO SEEMS FASCINATED BY "GAY BOYS" – HE MADE HOMOEROTIC PHOTOGRAPHY MAINSTREAM WITH THE SUPPORT OF CALVIN KLEIN – IT'S MY IMAGINATION I'M CERTAIN – BUT THESE PICTURES REMIND ME OF "HITLER YOUTH" – CIRCA 30's & 40's –

- 40'S – HIGH SCHOOL IS OVER – THANK YOU DEAR GOD – ONCE MORE I'VE BEEN SET FREE – WORLD WAR 2 IS OVER & SLOWLY SOME OF THE TRUTH COMES OUT – EVERYONE TURNED ON THE ORIGINAL OUTCASTS – THE JEWS – IN MY SMALL TOWN THE JEWS WERE BANNED FROM THE COUNTRY CLUB – THEY COULD NOT BUY LAND IN THE HAMPTONS – THEY NOW "OWN" THE HAMPTONS BABY – IN MY SENIOR YEAR I DATED ELEANOR PINCUS – SHE WAS SO BEAUTIFUL – ONE NIGHT SHE TOLD ME HER FATHER FORBADE HER FROM SEEING ME BECAUSE I WAS A GENTILE –

- 90'S – ONE DAY THE PHONE RANG & A TOTAL STRANGER INVITED ME TO A PARTY ON LONG ISLAND TO CELEBRATE THE 50TH REUNION ~~ANNIVERSARY~~ OF MY HIGH SCHOOL CLASS – HOW THE HELL DID THEY FIND ME – I DECLINED – THE PARTY WAS HELD AT THE COUNTRY CLUB –

— 40's — ENROLLING AT PARSON'S SCHOOL OF DESIGN WAS PERPLEXING — I TRIED & FAILED FASHION ILLUSTRATION — KEPT THINKING ABOUT GRAPHIC DESIGN & ARCHITECTURE — PARSON'S HAD WONDERFUL TEACHERS & LECTURERS — IT WAS JUST ONE BUILDING ON 57 ST — AND AN ANNEX IN LONG ISLAND CITY FOR FIRST YEAR STUDENTS — THIRD YEAR STUDENTS COULD STUDY IN PARIS — SO MANY TALENTED STUDENTS & STIFF COMPETITION — THE VERY BEST THING I HAVE EVER DONE IS TEACH — PERHAPS THAT'S THE REASON TEACHING MYSELF SEEMS TO BE THE ONLY WAY TO LEARN & THEN MASTER ANYTHING. LEAVING PARSON'S SEEMED A FAILURE — IT WAS A BLESSING — NEXT STOP WAS PRATT INSTITUTE IN BROOKLYN FOR GRAPHIC DESIGN CLASSES — HERE I LEARNED "SPACIAL RELATIONSHIP" BY STUDYING JAPANESE HOUSES & GARDENS — THE BEAUTY & POWER OF SIMPLICITY —

— 40's — MY FATHER WAS AN EXECUTIVE AT ABERCROMBIE & FITCH — ALL MY VERY PROPER CLOTHES CAME FROM THERE. IT WAS CONSIDERED MORE CONSERVATIVE THAN IT'S NEIGHBOR ON MADISON AVE — BROOK'S BROTHERS — EVERY PIECE OF CLOTHING WAS MADE IN ENGLAND — SCOTTLAND & IRELAND — WEARING BEAUTIFUL CLOTHES JUST LIKE MY FATHER ENDED WITH THE BEAT GENERATION — NOW THAT WAS A REVOLUTION BABY — MORE THAN CARNABY STREET FOR SURE — MY UNIFORM WAS A PEA COAT — DUNGAREES — WATCH CAP — BOOTS — YOU COULD GET IT ALL AT AN ARMY & NAVY STORE — LOW BUDGET CHIC — THE WHITE HORSE TAVERN & CAFE'S ON MULBERRY ST. WERE HANGOUTS — JUST BOOZE — NO DRUGS TILL THE LATE 50's — "HIP" WAS IN —

— 2003 — ARE AMERICA'S POLITICIANS COMING FROM CENTRAL CASTING OR ARE THEY BEING CLONED —

- 2003 - LABOR UNIONS SEEMED THE ONLY ANSWER TO MY FATHER - FROM COLLEGE TO MANAGEMENT WAS HIS ROUTE - LATER IN LIFE HE FELT THAT UNIONS WERE A NECESSARY EVIL - MANAGEMENT & UNION LEADERS CRAVED THE SAME POWER OVER THE WORKING STIFF - CORRUPTION IS A WAY OF LIFE - HE BELIEVED THAT WE ARE BORN TO WORK AND THE WILLING SHOULD BE TREATED WITH RESPECT - AMBITION LIVED IN HIS BONES -

- 90'S A GERMAN MAGAZINE ASKED ME TO PHOTOGRAPH TOM FORD - I SHOT HIM IN BED WITH HIS HANDS OVER HIS CROTCH - WHEN ASKED IF HE SMOKED WEED - HIS REPLY WAS "ONLY ON NIGHTS AND WEEKENDS" - HE HAD JUST TAKEN CHARGE AT GUCCI & I TOLD HIM TO WATCH HIS BACK - HE HAS A PHOTOGRAPH OF MINE IN THE LIVING ROOM OF HIS PARIS APARTMENT -

- 2003 – THE SOLE PURPOSE OF THE UNITED NATIONS IS TO OCCUPY SOME PRIME REAL ESTATE ON FIRST AVE. – SOMEDAY IT WILL BE A VEGAS STYLE HOTEL –

- 40'S – COMMUTING EVERY DAY FROM LONG ISLAND TO MANHATTAN ~~EVERY DAY~~ WAS NOT EASY – LIVING IN THE VILLAGE WAS A GOAL LIKE THOUSANDS OF YOUNG PEOPLE FROM ALL OVER THE U.S. – CARRYING A PORTFOLIO OF DRAWINGS AND GETTING REJECTED BECAME A CONSTANT HUMILIATION – EVERY MORNING WHEN LEAVING – MY MOTHER WOULD SAY "STAND UP STRAIT" – LOOKING BACK I MARVEL AT MY PARENTS SUPPORT –

- 40'S – BRAVO M.G.M. – WHAT WONDERFUL MUSICALS – ALL IN GARISH TECHNICOLOR – GENE KELLY – FRED ASTAIR – SINATRA – LENA HORNE – JUDY GARLAND – AND THEN THE "B" PICTURES – LOW BUDGET –

BRILLIANT DIRECTORS + WRITERS — SOME EXTRAORDINARY ACTORS — BEING TOUGH — UNABLE TO SWEAR — KILLINGS WITH SMALL AMOUNT OF BLOOD — FEAR — TERROR — NIGHTIME L.A. STREETS — BRAVO FILM NOIR — EVERYTHING SHOT IN GLORIOUS BLACK + WHITE —

= 2003 — WHEN STUDENTS ASK ME WHAT INSPIRED MY PHOTOGRAPHY — THE ANSWER IS — MY LIFE — FROM EARLY CHILDHOOD TO OLD AGE — I HAVE ALWAYS PHOTOGRAPHED LONELINESS BECAUSE THAT IS MY LIFE — PEOPLE SAY MY WORK IS SEXUAL — LOOK CLOSER STUPID — JOAN BUCK + INGRID SISCHY HAVE SAID IN PRINT THAT MY WORK IS ALL ABOUT DOOM — LOOK CLOSER STUPID —

= 40'S — SPENDING TIME WITH THE GIRL I WOULD MARRY — DATES IN NEW YORK TRYING TO BE GROWN UP — GIRLS FROM GOOD FAMILIES DID NOT PUT OUT — A DIAMOND RING WAS REQUIRED — I COULD GO DOWN ON A GIRL — BUT NO SCREWING —

— 40'S — GOT JOBS DESIGNING FABRICS —
ALL FREE LANCE — IN THE FLAT
IRON BUILDING — DESIGNING WINDOW
DISPLAYS AT SAK'S FIFTH AVE. —
LEADING NOWHERE — SPENT SOME
TIME AT PARSON'S WITH CARRIE
DONOVAN — SHE LIVED IN QUEENS
WITH HER MOTHER — WORKED WITH
HER YEARS LATER WHEN SHE WAS
THE EDITOR OF HARPER'S BAZAAR —
MOST OF THE PHOTOS WERE KILLED —
CARRIE WAS A TRIP & A HALF —
SO MANY PEOPLE TRYING TO SPEAK
LIKE MRS. VREELAND — POLLY
MELLON DOES THE BEST IMITATION —
ANDY TALLEY DOES THE ABSOLUTE
WORST — IF YOU ARE AN ORIGINAL
YOU WILL NEVER COPY ANYONE —

— 2003 — THE MOST DANGEROUS PEOPLE
ON THIS PLANET ARE THOSE WHO
HAVE NOTHING TO LOSE —

— 50'S — THIS IS THE LAST DECADE
BEFORE THE REVOLUTION — TEN MORE
YEARS OF SUPERB TASTE & GOOD
MANNERS —

— 50's — ~~MARRIED~~ MARRIED BARBARA — WEDDING AT ST. AGNES CATHEDRAL — RECEPTION AT THE COUNTRY CLUB FOR THREE HUNDRED STRANGERS — MY OLDER BROTHER HAS DRUNKEN ~~FIST~~ FIGHT WITH BARBARA'S OLDER BROTHER — RENTED CAR — FIRST NIGHT AT ESSEX HOUSE ON CENTRAL PARK SOUTH — TWO WEEK HONEYMOON IN THE BEAUTIFUL POCONO MOUNTAINS — TWO YOUNG ADULTS MAKING A SERIOUS MISTAKE — SEX WAS GOOD — THIS BECAME MY FIRST EXPERIENCE WITH JEALOUSY — GOT SMALL PLACE IN WEST VILLAGE WITH A VIEW OF WONDERFUL OLD CHERRY LANE THEATER — AFTER THE SEXUAL REVOLUTION THE VILLAGE BECAME "BOYS TOWN" EAST — WEST HOLLYWOOD WAS NOT FAR BEHIND —

— 2003 — LAST NIGHT "ROCCO & HIS BROTHERS" WAS ON CABLE — VISCONTI ~~AGE~~ A GENIUS WHO ALLOWED LOW CLASS MEN TO PULL HIM DOWN — CLOSE UPS ON ALAIN DELON — A NO BUDGET MASTERPIECE —

= 50'S – KOREA TO THIS DAY HAS A TRAGIC HISTORY – "UNCLE SAM" SENT ME A "GREETINGS" LETTER – AN ARMY PHYSICAL CONCLUDED THAT A HEART MURMUR RENDERED ME A "4F" – THE WAR BETWEEN NORTH + SOUTH RAGED ON – ONE YEAR LATER AND ANOTHER LETTER FROM MY UNCLE HAD A DIFFERENT RESULT – NO MORE HEART MURMUR WON ME A "1A" RATING – SUDDENLY I WAS A G.I. – MY WIFE SAID A TEARFULL GOODBYE + BASIC TRAINING AWAITED – YEARS LATER THIS TRAINING EQUIPPED ME FOR STREET LIFE – YOU MUST HAVE SHELTER – FOOD + WATER =

= 2003 – NIETZSCHE SAID THAT IN LIFE THERE WAS NO GOOD OR EVIL – ONLY AN ENDLESS STRUGGLE TO SURVIVE –

= 50'S – WATCHING A NAPALM STRIKE WAS TRULY AWESOME – SOUTH KOREA'S ARMY WAS HAPPY TO

Let America's youngest do most of the grunt work — when the Chinese crossed the Yalu River they used "human wave" assaults + terror against the constantly retreating South Koreans — All Asians were called "Gooks" by the ~~G.I.'s~~ Americans — The sound of 50 caliber machine guns sending rounds over your head is not comforting — Dirty underwear — Blisters on your feet — "C" rations always had cigarets + chocolate for energy — In summer there was terrible heat + bugs — In the winter you slept in deep snow — Everyone around me suffered — ~~quietly~~ — My father sent me beautiful letters — reading between the lines there was so much love — but never that word — Everyone jerking off + lies about their prowess — Dead G.I.'s stacked like cordwood in the back of "deuce + a half" ton trucks driven to the rear — Will it ever end —

— 50'S — SENT TO TOKYO FOR REST + RELAXATION — MY HOTEL WAS THE IMPERIAL — DESIGNED BY FRANK LLOYD WRIGHT — (NOW GONE) IT WAS SO BEAUTIFUL — WE WERE ACROSS FROM THE WALLED IMPERIAL PALACE — GENERAL MACARTHUR RULED — HE WAS AN AMERICAN ARISTOCRAT + HAD GREAT CHIC — I STILL RECALL MY FIRST MEAL — TROUT COOKED IN CHAMPAGNE — I NEVER ROSE ABOVE PRIVATE — MET A YOUNG LIEUTENANT + TOGETHER WE WENT TO A BATHOUSE — YOUNG SMILING GIRLS WOULD BATHE YOU AND MASSAGE YOU BY WALKING ON YOUR BACK — FOLLOWED BY A JAPANESE BLOW JOB — BAUGHT A RICE PAPER SCROLL + AN OLD LACQUER BOX AND SENT IT HOME — RETURNED TO KOREA TO HEAR OF "PEACE TALKS" — THOUSANDS OF YOUNG MEN ON BOTH SIDES DIED WHILE THESE TALKS DRAGGED ON — BUT IT ENDED ONE HOT DAY IN JULY —

= 50'S — SIX MORE MONTHS OF GAURD DUTY & ROAD BUILDING NOW THAT THE WAR WAS OVER — DECIDED TO DO WHAT HUNDREDS OF OTHER "GET ME OUT OF HERE" SOLDIERS WERE DOING — TOLD AN ARMY PSYCHIATRIST THAT I WAS HOMOSEXUAL — THIS GUY GAVE ME A RORSHOCK TEST & THEN GOT ME A MEDICAL DISCHARGE = FREEDOM WAS A THIRTY DAY BOAT TRIP TO ~~SEATTLE~~ SEATTLE WASHINGTON — A FIVE DAY TRAIN RIDE TO NEW JERSEY — A TAXI TO NEW YORK CITY —

= 2003 — WHO IS MORE DANGEROUS = THE PETTY THIEF ~~WHO~~ STEALS YOUR WALLET — OR THE C.E.O. WHO STEALS YOUR LIFE SAVINGS =

= 50'S — DESIGNING MILITARY INSPIRED JACKETS BECAME A ~~HOBBY~~ — MADE SKETCH OF A JACKET FOR MY WIFE — SHE HAD A MEN'S TAILOR MAKE IT FOR HER —

= 2003 – THERE WAS A TANGERINE SUNRISE AT 6 AM – TOOK MY DOG FOR A WALK – COFFEE + CIGARETTES + THE L.A. TIMES – A SMALL TOWN NEWSPAPER FOR ONE OF THE LARGEST CITIES IN THE WORLD –

= 50'S – AFTER WE WERE MARRIED MY WIFE TOLD ME SHE STARTED SNEAKING BOOZE FROM HER FATHER'S BAR WHEN SHE WAS TEN YEARS OLD – SHE COULD DRINK ANY MAN UNDER THE TABLE WITH SOME DECORUM – WHILE OVERSEAS MY FATHER TOOK HER TO A REHAB CENTER IN CONNECTICUT – WHEN ARMY LIFE FINISHED SO DID MARRIED LIFE – THE FASTEST WAY TO PUSH A MAN AWAY IS TO SURRENDER TO JEALOUS RAGES –

= 50'S – SHORTLY AFTER HER WEDDING MY SISTER WENT THROUGH THE WINDSHIELD – SHE IS STILL ON DRUGS – IN THE

60'S MY SECOND WIFE WAS CRIPPLED IN HER CAR ON A HOLLYWOOD FREEWAY - IN THE 70'S MY MOTHER DIED IN AN ACCIDENT ON LONG ISLAND -

- 50'S - MY FATHER IN LAW HAD ONE OF THE FIRST TELEVISION SETS IN TOWN - THERE WERE SOME BRILLIANT PLAYS DONE LIVE - T.V. COMMERCIALS WERE ALSO LIVE - HOLLYWOOD WAS TERRIFIED - AS USUAL ~~PEOPLE~~ PEOPLE WERE SURE IT WOULDN'T LAST -

- 50'S - A MAN NEVER LEAVES A WOMAN WHO MAKES HIM HAPPY - WHEN YOU LEARN LATER THAT YOUR EX IS PREGNANT IT IS EVEN SADDER - SHE TOOK FERTILITY DRUGS - MY DAUGHTER WAS NAMED MAGGIE -

- 50'S - WHY DID SUICIDE SEEM THE ONLY WAY TO STOP THE ELECTRIC STORM IN MY HEAD - THERE WOULD BE THREE MORE SUICIDE ATTEMPS WITH THIS

DIFFERENCE – THEY BECAME VIOLENT ONCE MORE WITH PILLS IN L.A. & TWICE I TRIED SLASHING MY WRISTS IN NEW YORK – AFTER EACH TRY THERE WOULD BE A CONFINEMENT IN A MAD HOUSE – PAYNE WHITNEY IS CHIC – BUT IT IS STILL A GENTEEL ASYLUM – TERRIBLE THINGS HAPPEN IN MENTAL HOSPITALS – WHOEVER INVENTED THORAZINE SHOULD BE HORSEWHIPPED – MY SECOND WIFE WENT TO CARTIER AND BOUGHT TWO WIDE LEATHER CUFFS WITH GOLD BUCKLES – WHY BOTHER – EVERYONE KNEW & NO ONE CARED – THE NEW YORKER DID A PIECE ON ME IN THE 90'S & ASKED IF ANYONE HELPED ME – EVEN MY PARENTS BACKED OFF – THEY WERE AFRAID OF ME & ASHAMED – THEY HAD TWO SONS WHO WERE SCHITZOPHRENIC – MY BIG – BRAVE BROTHER GAVE IN TO IT – I FAUGHT BACK & WON – IT TOOK TWENTY TERRIFYING YEARS –

— 2003 – ANYONE WITH A SECRET LIVES IN FEAR – I DON'T GIVE A FUCK WHAT ANYONE THINKS OF ME – I KNOW THAT POSESSING A GOD GIVEN TALENT PUTS ME AHEAD OF THOSE WHOSE LIVES ARE SPENT INSIDE THEIR OWN CASH REGISTER – MAKING BEAUTY WITH ONE'S HANDS & IMAGINATION CANNOT BE TRUMPED. WHAT THE HELL WOULD I DO WITH A LOT OF MONEY – GIVING IT AWAY WOULD BE THE ONLY ANSWER –

— 50'S – JAZZ NEVER MOVED ME – COOL JAZZ & BEBOP WAS VERY CEREBRAL – YOU CAN WORK UP A SWEAT OVER ROCK – LIKE EVERYONE IN MY GENERATION SINATRA WAS THE "VOICE" – CAN ANYONE NOT BE MOVED BY LADY DAY – DRESSED IN WHITE WITH CONKED HAIR & GARDENIAS – HEROIN SLOWING THIS GREAT VOICE – "SCAT" SINGING BY ELLA FITZGERALD – SARAH VAUGHAN – LENA HORNE CARRIED ON STAGE

BY TWO MEN BECAUSE HER DRESS WAS TOO TIGHT — NOEL COWARD + MARLENE DIETRICH TALK-SINGING IN LAS VEGAS — AND TOWARD THE END HERE COMES JERRY LEE LEWIS — LITTLE RICHARD + FINALLY ELVIS TO GIVE THE WORD "GROOVE" A NEW NAME — ROCK — ART DOSEN'T CHANGE TILL IT HAS TO — THE CRITICS WHO WRITE ABOUT ART ARE GROUPIES OR SABOTUERS — TODAY'S CRITICS ARE "STAR FUCKERS" — JOURNALISTS REVEAL MORE ABOUT THEMSELVES THAN THE ARTISTS THEY STUGGLE TO PROFILE —

— 50'S — DESIGNING LEXINGTON AV. WINDOWS FOR "BLOOMIES" — DOING ANY FREELANCE WORK I CAN GET — A FRIEND WANTS TO DRIVE SOUTHERN PACIFIC ROUTE TO L.A. SHOULD I GO — WHY NOT — FUCKING + SUCKING WAS OVERCOMING ME — ENOUGH BOOZE + I WOULD TRY ANYTHING — EVERY AMERICAN SHOULD DRIVE ROUTE 66 FROM CHICAGO TO L.A.

– 50'S – WHILE I WAS IN L.A. A FRIEND GAVE ME A CAMERA – A BEAUTIFUL ROLIFLEX – BEING A PAINTER THE FIRST PHOTOGRAPH I TOOK WAS A STILL LIFE – I NEVER PAINTED AGAIN – STILL IN L.A. MY FRIEND INTRODUCED ME TO A GIRL WHO WAS DANCING IN A ROAD COMPANY OF A BROADWAY MUSICAL – HER NAME WAS NORMA – BACK IN NEW YORK SHE MOVED IN WITH ME – SHE WAS A SHOWGIRL AT THE COPACABANA + THEN A BROADWAY MUSICAL –

– 90'S – THE "FACE" MAGAZINE ASKED MY SON TO PHOTOGRAPH CALVIN KLEIN – HE SHOT HIM SITTING ON THE TOILET WITH THE LID DOWN – THERE ARE EXTRA ROLLS OF TOILET PAPER ON THE TANK BEHIND HIM – MR. KLEIN'S LAWYER TOLD THE FACE NOT TO PUBLISH THE PHOTOGRAPH – THE MAGAZINE KILLED IT SO AS NOT TO LOSE ADVERTISING REVENUE – THAT IS CENSORSHIP – MR. KLEIN complained to me at a dinner party that he was censored for promoting "Heroin Chic" + "Pedofile Chic" — my son is an artist + was braught up in New York — Paris — Woodstock + L.A. Mr. Klein is a "Garmento" who was braught up in the Bronx —

≡ 50's — I met Carmen (extraordinary model for Avedon) + she got me an assistant's job working for her boyfriend (Dick Heyman) who was a second rate photographer = but he was great looking + the models loved him — he took a bath in Joy perfume + smoked Gauloise cigarettes — his tantrums gave the word Prima Donna new meaning — China Machado + Deborah Dixon did test shots for me — I learned dark room technique from his other assistant — after six months I told him to go fuck himself + left — I had learned all I needed to know —

⇒ 60'S — THE CULTURAL & SEXUAL REVOLUTION TOOK PLACE IN LONDON & NEW YORK — IT ~~SPREAD~~ SPREAD LATER TO L.A. — LATER STILL TO ROME — AND THEN THE WORLD — PARIS WAS TOTALLY OBLIVIOUS TO CHANGE OF ANY KIND WITH THE EXCEPTION OF THEIR CINEMA ⇐

⇒ 60'S — SEX OF EVERY KIND — ACID & WEED — ROCK MUSIC — ASSASSINATIONS — VIETNAM — DRUG OVERDOSES — WOMEN & GAYS WERE LIBERATED — CIVIL RIGHTS — POP ART — OP ART — FASHION FROM THE STREET — "EASY RIDER" — "TAXI DRIVER" — ANDY WARHOL — ST. TROPEZ — MARAKESH — TANGIER — BOB DYLAN — SGT. PEPPER — JANICE JOPLIN — JIMI HENDRICKS — HAIGHT ASHBURY — MICK JAGGER & KEITH RICHARDS — GROUPIES — DANCING ALONE — PEACE MARCHERS IN THE MILLIONS — C.I.A. — THE DISCO "PEPPERMINT LOUNGE" — BLACK PANTHERS — HAIRDRESSERS — CULT STAR CHARLES MANSON — "BREATHLESS" — FELLINI — PASOLINI —

DR. FEELGOOD — SPEED — DIANE ARBUS — "BONNY & CLYDE" — THE NIKON — THE "BEAUTIFUL PEOPE" — EDIE SEDGWICK — LIMOS — MINI SKIRTS — BELL BOTTOMS — "GROOVIE" "DO YOUR OWN THING" — "LET IT ALL HANG OUT" — VIET CONG — JACK & JACKIE STAR IN CAMELOT — LA CIENEGA BLVD. — SURFING — "THE IN CROWD" — GRANNIE TAKES A TRIP — DAVID BAILEY — COCKNEY CHIC — TWIGGY — JOSEPH LOSEY — TONY RICHARDSON — TERRY STAMP — PSYCADELIC — SKINHEADS IN LONDON — PLAYBOY — THE FILMORE — HELL'S ANGELS — WOODSTOCK — JIM MORRISON — FUNKIE — FIRE ISLAND — GROUP SEX — WIFE SWAPPING — "BLOW UP" — ANTONIONI — "LA DOLCE VITA" — THE PAPPARAZI — BARDOT — BELMONDO — JET SET — AND AT HARPER'S BAZAAR BOB RICHARDSON TAKES OVER — IT'S THE WOMAN THAT COUNTS — NOT THE CLOTHES —

60'S — SHEILA METZNER WAS AN ART DIRECTOR AT ~~HERPER~~ DOYLE-DANE-BERNBACH AD AGENCY — SHE TOLD ME THAT I WAS BLACKLISTED & ASKED IF I KNEW WHAT THE WORD "CABAL" MEANT — HOW COULD I —

= 60'S — ~~[illegible]~~ WE HAD A SMALL APARTMENT ON CHARLES ST. — DEBORAH DIXON & DONALD CAMELL ACROSS THE WAY — DONALD WROTE & DIRECTED "PERFORMANCE" UNTIL HE WAS REPLACED BY NICK ROEG HIS CAMERAMAN — YEARS LATER AFTER A BAD EXPERIENCE WITH MARLON BRANDO — DONALD SHOT HIMSELF IN THE HEAD — DONALD LOVED THREESOMS & SO DID I —

= 60'S — MARVIN ISRAEL WAS A GENIUS — AN EXCELLENT PAINTER & PHOTOGRAPHER — HE WAS A DIFFICULT ART DIRECTOR — VERY DEMANDING — I LOVED HIM — SEEING EVERY WITH ONE NEW

PHOTOGRAPH EACH TIME FINALLY WORE DOWN HIS RESISTANCE — HE GAVE ME THE LAST PAGE OF THE EDITORIAL SECTION TO SHOOT — HE THEN MADE ME RESHOOT THE PHOTO — HE DEMANDED I MAKE IT STRONGER — AND THE PHOTOGRAPH MEANT I HADN'T FAILED HIS TEST — MARVIN HAD TWO YOUNG ASSISTANTS — RUTH ANSEL & BEA FEITLER —

— 60's — MEETING ANNA PIAGI & HER HUSBAND — PHOTOGRAPHER ALFA CASTALDI — WAS A WONDERFUL EXPERIENCE FOR A PHOTOGRAPHER WHO NEEDED A GENIUS EDITOR — OSCAR WILDE MEANT MY PAL ANNA WHEN HE SAID " IF YOU CAN'T CREATE A WORK OF ART — BE ONE" — WE SHOT YVES ST. LAURANT COUTURE ON ANJELICA HUSTON — SERGE LUTENS DID THE MAKEUP — WE WORKED IN A SMALL STUDIO IN PARIS — WE DRANK BOTTLES OF RED WINE — THE PHOTOS WERE DONE FOR ITALIAN VOGUE —

60's — NORMA — THE GIRL I LIVED WITH — WOULD BECOME MY SECOND WIFE + TERRY'S MOTHER — SHE WAS VERY TOUCHING — HER FAVORITE WORD WAS "NEVER" — SHE HAD HER "TOO JEWISH" NOSE DONE + USED RICHARDSON AS HER STAGE NAME — SHE SAID JEWISH MEN WERE "MOMMA'S BOYS" + WOULD NEVER MARRY ONE — SHE DECIDED NOT TO WORK AS AN ACTRESS + SPENT HER TIME IN MY STUDIO ON 58 ST + 10TH AVENUE — WE HAD THE 2ND FLOOR THROUGH TWO BUILDINGS — SHE DIDN'T SEEM TO CARE THAT I WAS MENTALLY ILL WITH TWO SUICIDE ATTEMPS BEHIND ME — SEX WAS GOOD BUT NOT GREAT FOR BOTH OF US —

60's — MARVIN WAS FIRED BECAUSE HE WAS TOO GOOD — MRS. VREELAND LEFT + WENT TO VOGUE — EVERY PHOTOGRAPHER FOUND RUTH + BEA A PROBLEM — THESE TWO VERY GIFTED GIRLS REPLACED ONE MAN — BAZAAR SLOWLY FELL APART —

— 60'S — WHEN "DOCTOR FEELGOOD" DECIDED TO ADOPT ME — MY LIFE BECAME A NIGHTMARE — IT WAS MY FAULT — FOR A WHILE A SPEED HIGH WAS A RUSH — LIKE ALL DRUGS — YOU NEED MORE + MORE SPEED TO SEND YOU UP — YOU NEED MORE + MORE CHAMPAGNE TO BRING YOU DOWN — SLEEPING TWO HOURS A NIGHT FOR MONTHS WAS TAKING A TERRIBLE TOLL —

— 60'S — IN THE GOOD DOCTOR'S OFFICE THERE WAS A LARGE PORTRAIT OF PRESIDENT KENNEDY — IT WAS PLACED OVER HIS WORK TABLE — MARK SHAW WAS A GOOD PHOTOGRAPHER WHO WAS WHITE HOUSE CAMERA MAN — SHOOTING THE BEAUTIFUL YOUNG KENNEDYS + THEIR KIDS — MARK WAS AN EARLY VICTIM OF SPEED — HE WAS FOUND DEAD WITH A NEEDLE IN HIS ARM — JERRY TROTTA (MARK'S EX) WORKED AT BAZAAR — SHE + I WERE ASKED BY THE NEW YORK TIMES TO cooperate on an exposé of this evil doctor — he ~~was a~~ lost his license — he was the first of a long list of "star fuckers" that I would encounter — how pathetic these creatures are —

— 2003 — Terrell Moore is a close friend — a painter & photographer — young & good looking — a stud for the ladies — his studio is out near the airport & is as large as a hangar — worked last night editing his film — we smoked some weed & opened a bottle of "red" — later we had dinner in Venice & went to a boring gallery opening — me & my dog slept on one of his many sofas — drove home at 6 AM — breakfast in Los Feliz —

— 70's — we were temporarily living at the Chelsea Hotel — big fight with Anjelica — she slashed one of her wrists — a doctor stiched

HER WRIST WITHOUT ANESTHETIC — AVOIDING FILING A POLICE REPORT FOR ATTEMPTED SUICIDE — ANOTHER DAY WE CAME HOME FROM MY STUDIO TO FIND A HEROIN ADDICT HIDING IN THE CLOSET — GAVE HIM ENOUGH MONEY FOR A FIX —

— 60'S — DR. JACOBSON WAS INTRODUCING FRANCO ZEFFERELLI TO ME AT THE MET OPERA HOUSE AS ANOTHER "PATIENT" — HE INTRODUCED ME TO STASH RADZIWILL IN LONDON AT AN EMBASSY WHERE THE "GOOD DOCTOR" WAS GIVEN A MEDAL — HE ASKED ME TO PHOTOGRAPH HIM WITH RADZIWILL — I THREW THE FILM AWAY — STARTING TO HEAR VOICES AND HALUCINATING BADLY —

— 2003 — WHY DOES WAR SURPRISE SO MANY PEOPLE — DON'T THEY READ HISTORY — WHAT DO THEY THINK THE EXPRESSION "STAR WARS" MEANS — IT MEANS WAR ON OTHER PLANETS — THAT'S THE FUTURE —

- 70's – MY SON & ME VACATION IN HAITI – STAY AT "OLAFSON'S HOTEL" – STAGGERING POVERTY – THIS IS HOW BLACK PEOPLE TREAT OTHER BLACK PEOPLE – VOODOO CEREMONIES ARE PRIMITIVE AND STUPID – HAD AN UNFORGETTABLE MASSAGE THAT ENDED IN A POWERFUL ORGASM –

- 60's – NORMA GOES TO LONDON WITH ME – STAY AT THE DORCHESTER – GO SEE PEOPLE ABOUT WORK – FALLING IN LOVE WITH LONDON IS EASY – FALLING IN LOVE WITH THE BRITISH IS NOT – BACK TO NEW YORK – PLAN TO SPEND TIME IN LONDON TO WORK FOR VOGUE & SHOOT SOME ADVERTISING –

- 2003 – DOING A ~~GALLERY~~ SHOW IN A NEW GALLERY IN HOLLYWOOD – I'M GOING TO DO POSTERS WHICH CAN BE MASS PRODUCED – NEED MONEY AS USUAL –

— 60's — DESTROYING MY ENTIRE STUDIO SENT ME TO A PRIVATE HOSPITAL WHERE DR. JACOBSON WAS WELL KNOWN AND PROTECTED — FIRST TIME IN A PADDED CELL WEARING A STRAIGHT JACKET — MORE THORAZINE — NORMA REALLY SCARED THIS TIME — MAYBE WE SHOULD ALL MOVE TO PARIS — WE ~~FRANSFER~~ TRANSFER FUNDS — STORE FURNITURE AND NEGATIVES — BOOK A FLIGHT + GO.

— 2003 — PARIS IS EASY TO ADORE — BUT THE FRENCH AIN'T EASY — THEY ARE TERRIBLY PROUD OF BEING ~~FRENCH~~ — ANTI EVERYONE — IF YOU ARE ENGLISH OR AMERICAN YOU ARE ON THEIR HIT LIST — WORKING THERE WAS GOOD FOR ME — THE STREET — THE BARS — THE CEMETERY — THE CAFE'S — THE LOOK OF MY PHOTOGRAPHS CHANGED — THE BEST WORK EXPERIENCE I HAVE HAD ARE THE YEARS AT FRENCH VOGUE —

— 60'S — LIVING IN THE SIXTEENTH ARRONDISSEMENT WAS HOME FOR A FEW YEARS — I LOVED WALKING MY DOG IN THE PARK — BITTER COLD WINTERS — DARK UNTIL ALMOST NOON — WE BOUGHT A SMALL RED FIAT CONVERTIBLE JUST BIG ENOUGH FOR NORMA — TERRY — ~~& ~~ LUCKY — BOB & NORMA AGAINST THE WORLD —

≡ 2003 — YOU LEARN NOTHING FROM SUCCESS — YOU LEARN EVERYTHING FROM FAILURE —

— ~~70~~'S — WORKING IN ~~LONON~~ LONDON FOR VOGUE — ANJELICA & ME DO SOME HEAVY OPIUM — NODDING OUT MAKES PHOTOGRAPHING A CHALLENGE — SAW DOCTORS IN LONON — PARIS & NEW YORK HOPING TO MAKE HER PREGNANT — BUT SHE'S NOT ABLE —

— 90'S — MY DAUGHTER MAGGIE ASKS "WILL YOU HATE ME BECAUSE I'M A LESBIAN" — MY REPLY — "WILL

YOU HATE YOUR DAD BECAUSE HE IS BISEXUAL" — WE BOTH LAUGH — SEX HAS NOTHING TO DO WITH LOVE + EVERYTHING TO DO WITH SEX — PERIOD —

— 30'S — HAVE YOU EVER BEEN TO AN IRISH WAKE — MY GRANDMOTHER SARAH O'SULLIVAN FINALLY WENT TO HEAVAN MY FATHER THAUGHT — MY MOTHER TOLD US "THE OLD BIDDY WENT THE OTHER WAY" — LOTS OF HEAVY DRINKING AND SOME BEAUTIFUL IRISH SONGS — THE MEN IN ONE ROOM — THE WOMEN IN ANOTHER — I REMEMBER HER AS SHORT — RAMROD STRAIGHT + NO NONSENSE — SHE ALWAYS SMELLED OF POWDER + ROUGE — I CAN SEE HER NOW —

— 2003 — WHY WAS CRYING SO OUT OF THE QUESTION — EVERYTHING MOVES ME TO TEARS NOW — ESPECIALLY MUSIC — THE SIMPLE INNOCENSE OF MOST CHILDREN HAS THE SAME REACTION —

2003 – FIGHTING FOR SANITY IN AN INSANE WORLD WAS THE ONLY ANSWER – THE TRUTH ABOUT ONESELF IS FOUND BY BEING NAKED + WITHOUT A MASK – THIS TOOK AT LEAST TEN YEARS – EVERY DAY REALTY BECAME THE GOAL – STOPPING STRANGERS ON THE STREET + QUESTIONING THEM ABOUT WHAT I WAS SEEING + GETTING THEM TO AGREE THAT INDEED THAT'S WHAT THEY SAW TO MADE ME KNOW THAT I WAS NOT HALLUCINATING – THIS BECAME A DAILY ROUTINE UNTIL I COULD TRUST MYSELF – ONE DAY I REALISED THAT THE ONLY VOICE I HEARD WAS MY OWN – YOU DO NOT NEED DOCTORS AND THEIR TERRIBLE DRUGS – YOU NEED THE TRUTH – PRIDE IS THE ONLY THING TO GET YOU PAST SHAME – YOU MUST REALISE THAT LIFE IS ONE BIG LIE – YOU ARE LIED TO STARTING AT YOUR BIRTH – FUCK THAT –

- 2003 - MARIANNE FAITHFUL TOLD ANJELICA THAT I WAS NICE - BUT MY WIFE WAS A BITCH - HER EX HUSBAND HAD AN AFFAIR WITH THE WOMAN WHO WOULD SOON BE MY EX WIFE.

- 60's - IN PARIS DR. PIERRE BENSUSSON WAS MY DOCTOR - HE HELPED SAVE MY SON'S LIFE ONCE - TERRY'S NANNY LEFT A BOTTLE OF ORANGE FLAVORED ASPIRIN OUT & HE ATE TH CONTENTS - PIERRE RUSHED US TO AMERICAN HOSPITAL IN NEUILLY WHERE THEY PUMPED HIS THREE YEAR OLD STOMACH.

- 60's - PUTTING A PORTFOLIO OF WORK PUBLISHED BY FRENCH VOGUE TOGETHER WE MOVED BACK TO NEW YORK - WE HAD TWO STATEROOMS ON THE LAST ~~VOYAGE~~ VOYAGE OF THE LUXE "ILE DE FRANCE - ONE STATEROOM FOR NORMA AND ME & THE DOG - AND ACROSS THE WAY A STATEROOM

FOR TERRY + HIS NANNY — WHEN WE DOCKED IN NEW YORK WE DROVE OFF THE BOAT IN OUR RED FIAT — IT WAS THE END OF THE SIXTIES — MY LONELY-TERRIFYING TRIP INTO HELL WAS ABOUT TO BEGIN — I DIDN'T KNOW IT — THANK GOD —

— 70'S — WE TAKE A PENTHOUSE ON JANE ST. NEAR THE RIVER — GOING TO PARTIES + BRINGING HOME PEOPLE IS SOMETHING THAT IS GOING TO BREAK US UP — NORMA IS TEN YEARS YOUNGER THAN ME + FROM A DIFFERENT BACKGROUND — A FRIEND OF HER'S WITH THE SAME "SWINGING" LIFESTYLE IS FOUND MURDERED BY HER HUSBAND — FINDING WORK IS DIFFICULT BECAUSE OF MY REPUTATION — START WORKING AGAIN FOR HARPER'S BAZAAR — ONE DAY AN EDITOR CALLS TO ASK IF I WANT TO PHOTOGRAPH SEVENTEEN YEAR OLD ANJELICA HUSTON —

=70'S — NORMA + I BREAK UP — THE MORNING I MOVED OUT SHE TELLS ME THAT IF I LEAVE HER SHE'LL TELL TERRY I LEFT HIM — NO WOMAN WOULD PUNISH HER OWN CHILD BECAUSE SHE CAN'T PUNISH THIS YOUNG CHILD'S FATHER — YEARS LATER NORMA TOLD ME THAT SHE TOLD MY ~~SON~~ THAT I LEFT HIM BECAUSE I WANTED TO MAKE MOVIES WITH ANGELICA — NORMA KNEW THAT THREE YEARS BEFORE OUR BREAKUP I HAD TURNED DOWN THIS OPPORTUNITY AT WILLIAM MORRIS — "HELL HATH NO FURY LIKE A WOMAN SCORNED." NO MAN LEAVES A WOMAN HE LOVES — THERE IS A DIFFERENCE BETWEEN LEAVING + BEING DRIVEN AWAY —

=2003 — THE MAKING OF A FILM MEANS WORKING FOR A LONG TIME WITH THE SAME PEOPLE — IT MEANS DEALING WITH THE

MONEY PEOPLE — FILM IS AN ART FORM OVERRUN BY PEOPLE WHO SEE IT AS A WAY TO A LARGE — VULGAR HOUSE — SEVERAL CARS — TROPHY WIVES — CUBAN CIGARS — LESBIAN HOOKERS — PENILE IMPLANTS — PLASTIC SURGERY — PUBLICISTS — BODY GAURDS — ILLEGAL MEXICAN SERVANTS — MORONIC "MEETINGS" — ALL OF THESE DEAL MAKERS ARE "WHAT MAKES SAMMY RUN" — YOU DON'T NEED A STRONG WILL — YOU NEED A STRONG STOMACH —

— 70's — NORMA MEETS + MARRIES AN ENGLISH ROCK MUSICIAN WHO LOOKS LIKE A YOUNGER VERSION OF ME — SHE CHANGES HER NAME ONCE AGAIN — THEY MOVE TO WOODSTOCK — HER NEW NAME IS ANNIE — ONE OF HER FRIENDS CALLED TO INFORM ME THAT SHE IS ON HEROIN — WHEN CONFRONTED — SHE DENIES IT — TERRY TOLD A JOURNALIST THAT SHE HAD SEX WITH KRIS KRISTOFERSEN IN FRONT OF HIM — HE WAS FIVE —

⇒ 70'S — AFTER ABOUT FOUR YEARS ANJELICA + I PART. NEVER TOLD HER THAT I WAS SCHIZOPHRENIC — SHAME + FEAR SILENCE ANYONE WHO IS MENTALLY ILL — SHE WOULD HAVE UNDERSTOOD. IN TIME SHE + MY SON BECAME FRIENDS + STILL ARE. TRIED TO TEACH HER HOW TO WORK A CAMERA — HER BEST PHOTOGRAPHS WERE DONE BY DICK AVEDON — NOT ME —

⇒ 2003 — AVEDON CLAIMS TO HAVE BEEN THE BEST PHOTOGRAPHER IN THE 60'S — BULLSHIT — BOB RICHARDSON WAS — DESPITE OF OR BECAUSE OF BEING INSANE AND STRUNG OUT ON DRUGS I MANAGED TO DO PHOTOGRAPHS THAT ARE CONSIDERED ICONIC — BEING KNOWN AS THE "PHOTOGRAPHER'S PHOTOGRAPHER" MEANS I LEAD + THEY FOLLOW — I'M BROKE + THEY ARE RICH —

⇒ 70'S — ISOLATED + ALONE — AFRAID

TO GO OUT — KEEP THINKING SOMEONE WANTS TO KILL ME — TRY AGAIN TO KILL MYSELF — MY PARENTS ARE CALLED + TAKE ME OUT TO LONG ISLAND — ANOTHER DOCTOR + MORE THORAZINE — SEE SO MUCH PAIN IN MY FATHER'S EYES — MY MOTHER TELLS ME "ROB DARLING — YOU ARE A DREAMER" — THERE ARE TWO KIND OF PEOPLE — THE DREAMERS + THE SCHEAMERS" WHICH ONE ARE YOU —

≡ 2003 — FRED ALLEN SAID THAT LIVING IN LOS ANGELES IS WONDERFUL IF YOU ARE AN ORANGE —

≡ 70'S — ALEXANDER LIEBERMAN AND GRACE MIRABELLA AT AMERICAN VOGUE TRY TO HELP ME — HE WOULD CALL ME + TELL ME HOW BRILLIANT MY WORK WAS + THAT LIVING QUIETLY WAS SO IMPORTANT — HE WAS ELEGANT + ERUDITE + VERY MUCH IN CHARGE — HE WAS AN ARTIST — NOT A "FASHIONISTA" — THEY

DON'T WANT PEOPLE LIKE HIM AT VOGUE — HE WAS HEAD & SHOULDER'S ABOVE ANYONE WHO FOLLOWED HIM AT "CONDÉ NASTY" —

— 70'S — ONE WINTER NIGHT I TOOK OFF ALL MY CLOTHES & WENT OUT ON THE STREET — ALONE & NAKED — I TRIED TO SCREAM BUT I COULDN'T — IT'S AMAZING THAT NO ONE STOPPED ME —

— 70'S — COULDN'T WATCH TELEVISION BECAUSE THE PEOPLE INSIDE THAT BOX SEEMED TO BE TALKING TO ME — KEPT PRAYING THAT GOD WOULD LET ME DIE — MY CLOTHES SEEMED TO BE FALLING APART & THEY LOOKED DIRTY — AFRAID TO WALK MY DOG — SHE WAS A SAINT BERNARD I CALLED "LADY" — FOUND SOMEONE WHO LIVED IN MONTAUK WITH SMALL CHILDREN & LAND TO TAKE THIS BIG FOOL WHO LOVED ME SO MUCH — WILL NEVER FORGET SAYING GOODBYE —

— 70'S — WHY GO TO AN ORGY IF YOU ARE JUST GOING TO WATCH — WOMEN HAD THE PILL + DIDN'T HAVE TO RUSH INTO THE JOHN FOR THEIR DIAPHRAM — STRAIGHT PEOPE WERE "EXPERIMENTING" — IN THE DARK — IF YOU ARE GETTING GREAT HEAD — WHO CARES WHO IS GIVING IT — IN THE DARK — A WOMAN COULD TAKE TWO MEN + NOT KNOW WHO THEY WERE — MOST PEOPLE THINK THAT ALL GOOD SEX IS DIRTY + IMMORAL — POOR BABIES — ON THE FLIPSIDE — HERPES AND AIDS WERE JUST UP THE BLOCK —

— 2003 — IF YOU THINK FOR YOURSELF — IF YOU ARE SPECIAL — YOU NEVER JOIN A PARTY — A GANG — A CLICK — A GROUP — YOU GO IT ALONE — IN ALL OF THE ARTS THERE IS AN "IN CROWD" — BEFORE LONG THEY JOIN THE "OUT CROWD" — GREAT + SMALL — FUCK 'EM ALL — EVEN UGLY PEOPE LOVE TO BE PHOTOGRAPHED — THE CAMERA REPLACED THE PAINT BRUSH A LONG TIME AGO —

— 70'S — COULDN'T SEE THROUGH THE VIEWFINDER ON MY NIKON — COULDN'T FOCUS — HAD TO PUT MY CAMERA ON A TRIPOD AND HAVE MY ASSISTANT FOCUS FOR ME — JUST WATCH THE MODEL + HIT THE SHUTTER — LOOKING AT A CONTACT SHEET WAS TOUGH — THAT CAN'T BE MY WORK — KEPT ASKING MY ASSISTANT "AM I OK?" "ARE YOU SURE?" — "AM I SHARP" — FELT ASHAMED — HARD TO TALK — I NEED A GOD DAMN DRINK —

— 70'S — CAN'T WORK — HAVE TO FACTOR ALL MY BILLS — THE MONEY IS GONE — WHAT IS GOING TO HAPPEN TO ME — NEVER TOLD ANYONE — HOW COULD I — I WAS BOOKED FOR WORK + DIDN'T SHOW UP — EVERYONE KNEW — HAD TO ESCAPE — BUT SAT HOME ALONE — DIDN'T EAT — JUST DRANK — SCORING GRASS WAS TOO MUCH OF AN EFFORT — HAVE ALWAYS LOATHED DEALERS + THEIR LITTLE POWER PLAYS —

— 2003 — For years I've been telling people that America is having the biggest nervous breakdown ever recorded — China is watching + waiting — they know all about an experiment that fails — there's one billion of them + after four thousand years — patience is second nature —

— 60's — I cherished the times when my wife and the nanny were out — I would take my son into the studio — put on some music + project the film I shot against a white wall — he would sit in my lap + watch — his blonde hair smelled from baby shampoo + he always wore Doctor Denton pajamas — I would open some champagne and tell him what was on my mind — he was always quiet with me — every night in Paris he would lie on the sofa in my arms + watch a children's show about a bear —

— 60's — WHILE TAKING A SLEEPING CURE IN GARCHES (WEST OF PARIS) MY WIFE WOULD BRING MY SON TO SEE ME — HE WOULD RUN DOWN THE HALL WITH HIS LITTLE ARMS STRETCHED OUT YELLING "DADDY — DADDY" — THERE I WAS IN SILK PAJAMAS + A DRESSING GOWN FROM SULKA — THROUGH THE WINDOWS WE COULD WATCH THE SWANS ON A SMALL LAKE — EVERY MORNING A NURSE WOULD PUT ME IN A BATH TUB + MAKE ME CLEAN + SMELL GOOD — THEN BREAKFAST + A "PICTURE" — THANK GOD FOR THE FRENCH —

— 2003 — THE PROBLEMS OVER THE ABORTION ISSUE CAN ONLY BE SOLVED BY WOMEN — WHY ARE ALL THESE MEN INVOLVED — MOST WOMEN HAVE ABORTIONS BECAUSE OF SOME MAN WHO DOES NOT RESPECT OR FEEL THE NEED TO PROTECT WOMEN — GIVEN TIME A FETUS WOULD BE A BOY OR GIRL — THIS IS

JUST ONE MORE EXAMPLE OF AMERICAN MEN WHO ARE PUSSY WHIPPED MOMMA'S BOYS PRETENDING TO BE MACHO — IF YOU CAN'T GET PAST ADOLESENCE — YOU ARE DOOMED —

— 2003 — IT STRANGE TO LIVE IN L.A. — THIS IS THE FIRST CITY I'VE LIVED IN WHERE FEELING LIKE A FOREIGNER NEVER LEAVES ME — THESE ARE THE SADDEST RUDEST — MOST ILL MANNERED PEOPLE ON THIS PLANET — THEY LIVE UNDER FEAR + INTIMIDATION —

— 70'S — STUDIO 54 WAS A NIGHTLY HALLOWEEN PARTY — FRIENDS WHO WERE BLASTED BEHIND COCAINE WOULD HIRE A LIMO + OFF WE WOULD GO — THERE WERE ALWAYS HUNDREDS OF PEOPLE OUTSIDE — THEY WOULD NEVER GAIN ENTRY — BEING THERE — SURROUNDED BY PEOPLE FRANTIC FOR ATTENTION — MADE ME FEEL LONELY — + ILL —

—70'S — WENT TO ROME FOR HARPER'S BAZAAR — THE EDITOR WAS MY PAL IRIS BIANCHI — SHE STRUGGLED TO HELP ME — WILL ALWAYS BE GRATEFUL TO THIS BEAUTIFUL — ARISTOCRATIC LADY — THE HOTEL MANAGER DEMANDED THAT THE MODEL LEAVE — AFTER WORK SHE WOULD CRUISE — AND BRING BACK GUYS WHO WERE HUSTLERS OFF THE VIA VENETO — IT WAS GETTING ALMOST IMPOSSIBLE TO WORK — MY MIND BETRAYED ME — DEAR GOD WHAT HAVE I DONE — PLEASE SAVE ME BEFORE IT'S TOO LATE — IT WAS ALREADY TOO LATE —

—70'S — TRAPPED ALONE IN MY BEAUTIFUL APARTMENT — CALLING GRISTEDES MARKET TO SEND FOOD — LIVING ON CHAMPAGNE — COFFEE — STEAK — CIGARETTES — THE NIGHTS WERE SO DARK — ANOTHER SUICIDE ATTEMPT — SLASHING ACCROSS OLD SCARS — EVERYONE KNEW —

– 70's – WORKED WHEN ABLE IN A STUDIO USED BY PAUL HYMAN + ANNIE LIEBOWITZH – THERE WERE BIG MARIJUANA PLANTS THAT CLIENTS THOUGHT WERE FICUS TREES – THE "STAR" HAIRDRESSER WAS ARA GALIANT WHO HAD DINNER PARTIES WITH COKE FOR DESSERT – LATER ON HE SHOT HIMSELF TO DEATH IN A VEGAS HOTEL – HE TOLD EVERYONE THAT CHER + JACK NICKOLSON WERE CLOSE FRIENDS. BUT WHERE WERE THESE FRIENDS AT THE END –

– 70's – ART KANE WAS A BRILLIANT ART DIRECTOR + PHOTOGRAPHER – MY SON WOULD GO WITH ME TO ART'S LOVELY OLD COUNTRY HOUSE ON WEEKENDS – HE TAUGHT AT THE ART CENTER BEFORE BEING FIRED FOR SEXUALLY HARRASING ONE OF HIS PRETTY STUDENTS – THE ART CENTER IS A SCHOOL FOR ~~RICH~~ RICH KIDS IN PASADENA – THIS

(124)

REALLY NICE GUY SHOT HIMSELF TO DEATH —

- 2003 — WRITING THIS IS LIKE TAKING A SHOWER TO GET ALL THE DIRT OFF —

- 2003 — AN "HOMAGE" IS ACTUALLY A CHEAP KNOCKOFF —

- 70'S — PEOPLE BELEIVED THAT COCAINE WAS NOT ADDICTIVE — AFTER ALL COLE PORTER + TALLULAH BANKHEAD DID IT — SO DID FREUD — THE GOOD DOCTOR DIED FROM THROAT CANCER — TO KILL THE PAIN HE WAS GIVEN HEROIN — THINK OF ALL THE CASUALTIES BECAUSE OF "SNOW" — ONCE IN WOODSTOCK ANJELICA DID SOME COKE + I SLAPPED HER — I TOLD HER SPEED WAS MORE HARMFUL BUT COKE WAS A CLOSE SECOND — SHE FOUND OUT LATER ON HOW PROBLEMATIC THIS DRUG COULD BE —

— 70's — MY EX WIFE — MY SON & HER HUSBAND MOVED TO L.A. — HE TRIED VERY HARD TO MAKE IT IN THE MUSIC BUSINESS — HE TOLD ME HE THOUGHT MOST AMERICANS WERE MUTANTS — AFTER NORMA'S ACCIDENT SHE STRUGGLED SO HARD — PARTIAL AMNESIA & AN INABILITY TO WALK BECAME HER BIGGEST CHALLENGE — IN THE END SHE WAS ABLE TO WALK WITH A CANE — THIS ALL HAPPENED TO A DANCER — SHE WENT TO COURT & PROVED THAT SHE WAS MENTALLY COMPETENT & ABLE TO MANAGE THE MONEY SHE RECEIVED — THIS LADY HAS GUTS — THE PEOPLE WHO KNOW HER AS "ANNIE" NEVER MET THE SHOWGIRL WITH A "NEW YORK ATTITUDE" THAT I KNEW AS NORMA — HER FAVORITE EXPRESSION WAS "CUT THE BULLSHIT" — THE FASHION EDITORS WERE TERRORFIED OF HER — SHE TRIED TO PROTECT ME — WE DIDN'T UNDERSTAND MY INSANITY — OR THE DANGER —

→ 2003 — People who do makeup & hair for fashion sittings are sabatuers — a beautiful young girl will show up with clean hair & no makeup — after hours of gossip & giggles this beautiful girl emerges from the dressing room looking like a drag queen — that's when I say "NO" — take it all off or I won't shoot her — this is my photo — not yours — the editors would never admit that they were hustling for hair & makeup advertising — they always said her tortured hair & hooker makeup was "devine" — the photos were published with hair & makeup credits — no one questioned the fact that the girl had beautiful hair & no makeup — I was difficult because I love beautiful girls & felt sorry for drag queens — if you know what you are doing and

YOU ARE ALWAYS WORKING WITH PEOPLE WHO DON'T — THINGS CAN GET UGLY —

— 70'S — TERRY WOULD FLY BY HIMSELF TO NEW YORK TO SPEND SUMMERS WITH ME — THERE WAS ALWAYS A FATHER PACING AT KENNEDY AIRPORT WAITING FOR THIS EXTRAORDINARY BOY TO GET OFF A JET — ONE SUMMER HE CALLED FROM L.A. & TOLD ME HE DIDN'T WANT TO COME — WHAT WAS LEFT OF ME DIED —

— 2003 — PLEASE EXPLAIN WHY ONE MILLION BLACK PEOPLE WERE BUTCHERED BY OTHER BLACK PEOPLE IN RWANDA — THERE ARE BLACK SLAVES HELD IN SERVITUDE BY BLACK SLAVE HOLDERS IN SUDAN — WHY AREN'T THEIR "BROTHERS & SISTERS" IN AMERICA SPEAKING OUT — IF YOU WANT RESPECT BABY — YOU GOTTA EARN IT — DOESN'T ANYONE CARE ABOUT THE WOMEN & CHILDREN — THEY WERE BLACK —

⇒ 2003 — L.A. WINTER — MONSOON RAIN ALL DAY — THE NEWS IS REALLY PATHETIC — AMERICANS WHO LOATHE OTHER AMERICANS — WHY DO "PEACE" DEMONSTRATORS LOOK SO ANGRY — PEOPLE MARCHING + PERFORMING FOR THE TV CAMERAS LOTS OF THEM WEARING ~~XXXXX~~ "CARNIVAL" COSTUMES — ALL THESE PEOPLE IN ONE BIG HERD — WHO IS THE PIED PIPER —

⇒ 70'S — WALKING DOWN FIFTH AV — LOOKING DOWN — AFRAID TO LOOK AT PEOPLE — THEY FREIGHTEN ME — THE TELEPHONE HAS STOPPED RINGING — BEHIND ~~THE~~ IN MY RENT — GOT TO GET OUT OF HERE — WHAT SHALL I DO WITH HUNDREDS OF NEGATIVES — THIS ONE VOICE IN MY HEAD THAT'S NOT MY OWN — GETTING CHEAP WINE NOW — EATING BREAD SO I DON'T VOMIT — BORROW $800 FROM MY SISTER — HAVE ONLY A FEW DOLLARS AT CHASE BANK ON PARK AV — STUFF OLD ~~CASHERE~~ SWEATERS + JEANS IN ONE LARGE LOUIS VUITON BAG — NO CAMERAS ⇒

— 70's — My son was being cared for by his maternal grandmother who adored him — but could not discipline him — Norma would not allow my son to know my parents — more cruelty — in one stroke she would not allow her son to know his father or his grandparents — the fact that my parents viewed her as an unfit mother didn't help — my father wanted Terry to stay with him on Long Island believing he needed a man & not ~~no~~ two women who fought over him constantly — my mother felt he needed courage and strength and he was running wild — my parents could not find me — no one could — years later I found that there were people searching — there are thousands of people without identification living on the street like shadows —

— 2003 — My parents are buried side by side on Long Island — Were they perfect — Are you — I learned to love my father after his death — Part of regaining my sanity — the years of self examination — were spent remembering what kind of man Harry Joseph Richardson was — Big plus + Big minus — It simply didn't matter that he so loved his first born the same way I loved my son — We were both dazzled — He was always a father — never a friend — If there is any good in me at all it is due to this man — He kept his thoughts about each of us to himself — He never said "I love you" — It was weakness in me to want to hear that — Actions speak louder than words — I salute you Dad —

— 70's — If you want to get as far away from New York — & still be in the U.S.A. — California is it. Finished as a photographer & finished as a man — A one way ticket to L.A. seemed the only answer — From a penthouse to a park bench was a short trip — Everyone I worked with in N.Y. considered me difficult — Nobody knew there was a constant electric storm in my brain — Took a room near Western & Wilshire Blvd. — Very sweet landlady — Drank all day — Money almost gone — Too ashamed to call my son — Pawned a tank watch from Cartier & a ring Norma gave me in Paris — Got $150 for both — The watch cost thousands — One day the rent money was gone — Walked out leaving what little I had — The clothes on my back & a few dollars were all I had — Took a bus to Santa Monica & my new home — the beach.

- 2003 – MY FATHER TOLD US THAT WHEN AMERICA WAS LIBERATING FRANCE – THE GERMANS USED MUSTARD GAS AGAINST US – HOW MANY YOUNG MEN DIED A TERRIBLE DEATH IN THE TRENCHES – SOME THINGS NEVER CHANGE –

- 70'S – HAVING SURVIVED LIVING ON THE STREET FOR TWO YEARS – SHOWED ME HOW STRONG I REALLY AM – STRENGTH HAS NOTHING TO DO WITH MUSCLES & BRAVADO – IT TAKES GUTS – PERIOD – MY ARMY TRAINING – PLUS DESIRE – GOT ME THROUGH – YOU MUST UNDERSTAND MADNESS – IT'S VERY SEDUCTIVE – DISCOVERING THE PUBLIC LIBRARY IN SANTA MONICA GAVE ME THE INFORMATION I NEEDED – THERE IS A WEALTH OF LITERATURE ON "PARANOID SCHITZOPHRENIA" AVAILABLE & SOME OF IT IS DIFFICULT READING – MANY COLLEGES HAVE PUBLISHED RECENT FINDINGS – I HAD NOTHING BUT TIME TO STUDY –

— 60'S — ONE DAY AT ORLY AIRPORT IN PARIS A YOUNG—TOO EAGER YOUNG MAN APPROACHED ME — HE TOLD ME HE WOULD ASSIST ME FOR NO SALARY IF I WOULD ONLY LET HIM WATCH ME WORK — BEFORE BOARDING A PLANE FOR LONDON HE WAS TOLD THAT THERE IS NOTHING TO LEARN ABOUT TAKING PICTURES + EVERYTHING TO LEARN ABOUT HIMSELF — HIS NAME WAS ARTHUR ELGORT — HE IS STILL IN THE DARK —

— 70'S — ONE NIGHT TEMPTATION OVERCAME COMMON SENSE — SITTING AT THE COUNTER OF A COFFEE SHOP + ORDERING SOUP + BREAD IN A WARM — BRIGHTLY LIT JOINT — A FANTASY WAS FULFILLED — WHAT WOULD THEY DO IF TOLD THEM ~~MY~~ MY POCKETS WERE EMPTY — THEY HAD ME BUSTED + SPENDING THE FIRST WARM — SAFE NIGHT IN A JAIL CELL WAS NOT A PUNISHMENT — IT GETS COLD AS HELL AT NIGHT IN SANTA MONICA —

- 70'S — MY TEETH BEGAN TO FALL OUT — IF YOU ARE HOMELESS — A GOOD DENTAL SURGEON IS OUT OF THE QUESTION — I READ ONCE THAT AMPHETEMINE ADDICTION MIGHT CAUSE THIS —

- 2003 — A GREAT ROCK + ROLL SOUNDTRACK ONLY HELPS A FILM IF YOU CAN GET UP + DANCE TO IT —

- 2003 — IT IS MORONIC TO THINK YOU CAN CHANGE THE WORLD — YOU CAN'T CHANGE HUMAN NATURE — WAKE UP —

- 2003 — WATCHED "ALL ABOUT EVE" ON CABLE LAST NIGHT — EVERY YOUNG ACTRESS IN HOLLYWOOD SHOULD STUDY THIS EXTRAORDINARY ARTIST — SHE WASN'T LIKE THEM — SHE KNEW HOW TO WORK A CAMERA — SHE COULD BE BEAUTIFUL OR UGLY — SHE WAS ALWAYS BETTE DAVIS — THE FACE — THE VOICE — THE CIGARETTE — THE BEST ACTRESS THAT EVER WORKED — SHE WILL NEVER BE TOPPED —

- 70's — ANJELICA I WENT TO DAVID BAILEY'S HOUSE IN LONDON — PENELOPE TREE — HIS LATEST GIRL — TOLD ME THAT DAVID BELIEVED THAT I WAS A BETTER PHOTOGRAPHER THAN HIM — WHO THE HELL WASN'T — THE GIRLS WENT OUT FOR A SHORT WHILE & DAVID STARTED "COMING ON" WITH ME — GROPING & FUMBLING — HIS REPUTATION WAS THAT OF A COCKNEY STUD WITH THE LADIES — WHEN THE GIRLS CAME BACK — WE ALL WENT OUT FOR DINNER — THE ENGLISH ARE SUCH DEVILS —

- 2003 — THERE WAS A PIECE IN THE L.A. TIMES BEGGING THE QUESTION IF THE JEWS CONTROL THE ENTIRE ENTERTAINMENT INDUSTRY — WHY DON'T THEY SPEAK OUT IN TOTAL SUPPORT FOR ISRAEL — THE ANSWER WAS "THE BOTTOM LINE" — I HAVE NEVER BEEN TO ISRAEL — BUT I THINK THESE PEOPLE ARE VERY IRISH —

– 70's – LIVING ON THE STREET FOR TWO YEARS SAVED MY LIFE BECAUSE I HAD TO BE REBORN – THE FIRST YEAR WAS A DRUNKEN DELERIUM – WANDERED THE STREETS OF VENICE ALL NIGHT – EVERY MORNING I WOULD ~~PANHANDLE~~ PANDHANDLE FOR ENOUGH MONEY FOR WHITE PORT WINE + CIGARETTES – I STOLE FOOD OR ATE OUT OF THE DUMPSTERS BEHIND THE RESTERAUNTS ON MAIN STREET. CROSSING THE FOOT BRIDGE OVER PACIFIC COAST HIGHWAY + ~~SETTLED~~ SITTING BENEATH A PALM TREE MY STUDIES WOULD BEGIN – THE BIG – PURE WHITE BIRDS WOULD COME IN + HOVER OVER ME – THEN MOVING THEIR WINGS BACKWARD – THEY WOULD TAKE BREAD FROM MY HAND + I COULD SEE THEIR EYES – THEY WERE NOT AFRAID OF ME – THEY WERE FREE – THEY COULD GO WHERE THEY WANTED TO – BUT ALWAYS ALONG THE COAST + OVER THE SEA – DIVINE –

— 70'S — FILTHY DIRTY — COVERED IN AN OLD BLANKET — STANDING QUIETLY — NO ONE SAW ME — ONE DAY A WOMAN HAD ME WAIT OUTSIDE A CAFE WHILE SHE HAD THEM PUT A HOT LUNCH TOGETHER — SHE SAT ON A BENCH WITH ME + TALKED ABOUT EGYPT — HER NATIVE COUNTRY — SHE WAS SO CLEAN — SHE TOLD ME THAT MY FACE REMINDED HER OF SOMEONE — MY STOMACH HURT FROM LENTIL SOUP + BROWN BREAD — I THANKED HER + SHE WAS GONE — SHE STAYED LONG ENOUGH TO BE SURE I ATE —

— 2003 — IS THERE A DIFFERENCE BETWEEN A HOLLYWOOD MOGUL + A HOLLYWOOD MONGREL — NEITHER ONE HAS A PEDIGREE —

— 70'S — EVERY DAY ON THE BEACH I WOULD KNOCK BACK MY WHITE PORT + SLEEP — IT WAS ONLY WHEN I WAS SOBER THAT I WOULD DREAM — + THEN — NIGHT

– 70's – STEALING SCISSORS + A RAZOR WAS EASY – GOD MUST HAVE BEEN WATCHING OVER ME – SOME KIND PERSON GAVE ME SOAP + A CLEAN TOWELL – THERE'S AN OUTDOOR SHOWER FOR BEACHGOERS TO WASH OFF SAND – DOWN ON THE BEACH AT FIVE IN THE MORNING I STRIPPED AND TOOK AN ICE COLD SHOWER – SOAPING OVER + OVER AGAIN – I WASHED MY SHIRT + UNDERWEAR + LET IT DRY ON THE SAND – BEING COLD SOBER AND CLEAN — PLANS WERE MADE – I SHAVED + CUT MY HAIR WITHOUT A MIRROR – ROAMING VENICE LATE AT NIGHT + FINDING A LAUNDRY BAG FULL OF "T SHIRTS" + SHORTS IN THE BACK OF AN UNLOCKED CAR – ALL THAT SOLVED PLAN ONE – FINDING AN EMPTY BACK PACK IN A GARAGE SOLVED PLAN TWO – HUSTLE SOME MONEY FOR BREAKFAST AT McDONALDS – THAT WAS THE LAST TIME I BEGGED OR STOLE – PRAYED TO MY FATHER –

— 70's — WALKED TO THE UNEMPLOYMENT OFFICE IN SANTA MONICA — A BIG — BLACK — BEAUTIFUL WOMAN INTERVIEWED ME — SHE KNEW I WAS HOMELESS — SENT ME TO AN OFFICE NEARBY WHERE THEY NEEDED HUGE BOXES OF FILING CARDS SORTED A TO Z — GETTING PAID IN CASH + BEING ABLE TO BUY DINNER AT A COFFEE SHOP WAS A RELIGIOUS EXPERIENCE — ~~THREE CUPS OF CO~~ — NOW — FIND A PLACE TO SLEEP WITH MY BACK AGAINST A WALL — MY SECOND YEAR BEGINS —

— 2003 — SOME PEOPLE THINK THAT ORGANISED RELIGION IS MORE DANGEROUS THAN THE MILITARY INDUSTRIAL COMPLEX — WHAT DO YOU THINK — CAN YOU THINK —

— 70's — MY PAL AT THE UNEMPLOYMENT OFFICE SCORES ME A JOB AS A DELIVERY DRIVER FOR A FLORIST — BY SOME MIRACLE MY WALLET SURVIVED WITH MY NEW YORK

DRIVER'S LICENSE & SOCIAL SECURITY CARD — WORKED EVERY AFTERNOON DELIVERING UGLY FLORAL ARRANGEMENTS TO MALIBU — NOT ONCE DID I GET A TIP — BOUGHT A SLEEPING BAG & A DUFFLE FOR MY NEW SECOND ~~JEANS~~ HAND JEANS & JACKET — SLEPT AT NIGHT ON A SIDE PORCH AT A SMALL PRIVATE SCHOOL NEAR THE BEACH — EVERY MORNING A COLD SHOWER & CLEAN CLOTHES DOWN ON AN ~~EEE~~ EMPTY BEACH — BREAKFAST AT A COFFEE SHOP & THEN A LONG WALK TO WORK — HID MY STUFF BEHIND A WALL AT THE SCHOOL — STARTED SAVING A FEW DOLLARS EACH WEEK — STARTING TO FEEL HUMAN AGAIN — REMEMBERING MY MOTHER SAYING "STAND UP STRAIGHT DARLING" —

— 70'S — NOT ONCE DID I THINK ABOUT PHOTOGRAPHY — SOMETIMES I WOULD TAKE A STICK & MAKE DRAWINGS IN THE SAND —

- 70'S — GOT ANOTHER JOB DELIVERING RECORDS + SMALL PACKAGES EVERY MORNING — WITH BOTH JOBS I WAS SAVING MORE EACH WEEK — DECIDED THAT WHEN I SAVED $500 GREYHOUND WOULD TAKE ME UP TO SAN FRANCISCO — A GYPSY KEEPS MOVING —

- 70'S — IT WAS MY DIFFICULT — ANGRY SON WHO WOULD MOVE TO SAN FRANCISCO + ONCE AGAIN PHOTOGRAPHY WOULD OVERCOME ME.

- 70'S — WHEN YOU ARE DRUNK ALL THE TIME SEX NEVER THUNKS YOU — WHEN YOU ARE SOBER AGAIN — SEX RETURNS + IT IS "RUSH CITY" —

- 80'S — THE FIRST TWO NIGHTS IN SAN FRANCISCO I SLEPT BEHIND CITY HALL — JOINED THE Y.M.C.A. FOR $25 A WEEK + TOOK A SHOWER THERE EACH DAY + LOOKED FOR WORK — GOT A JOB MY FIRST DAY OUT AS A TELEPHONE SOLICITOR — THE SECOND day I found a room in Chinatown — the first night with a ceiling rather than the stars over my head was another emotional triumph — lived in this anchient hotel for five years — one day I realised that my sanity was coming back — being able to work at anything with a peacefull mind humbeled me — no one helped me — I did it all on my own — at night drinking "Dago Red" just enough to mellow me out — the Chinese fascinated me — they are such hard workers + very "la familia" —

— 2003 — critics are totally useless — ~~people~~ people can read a book — see a movie — listen to music — go to a museum without their help — people can form their own opinions — why not send them to university + let them find a real job — think I'll take my dog for a walk + chill —

- 2003 - Saw a photo in the L.A. Times of Anjelica leading a "peace" demonstration - had no idea she attended intelligence briefings every morning - does she know that an actress in Baghdad speaking out like that would be killed - last year she was quoted saying that President + Mrs. Clinton have an ideal marriage -

- 70's - Called my older brother who was living in San Diego - went to stay with him for a short stay - he was heavily sedated with Haldol - when it came time to leave he pleaded with me stay + take care of him - never spoke to him again - living in New York in the 90's I would see him on the street looking beaten - he never saw me -

- 80's - Living in San Francisco's Chinatown was a hiding place -

THERE WAS A KNOCK ON MY DOOR ONE DAY FROM MARTIN HARRISON — HE TOLD ME HE WAS MY ASSISTANT AT THE VOGUE STUDIO IN LONDON DURING THE SIXTIES — HE WAS PRODUCING A BOOK ON THE HISTORY OF FASHION PHOTOGRAPHY & THAT DICK AVEDON REFUSED TO PARTICIPATE UNLESS MY WORK WAS INCLUDED — HE DID NOT INCLUDE THE WORK OF STEVEN MEISEL, WHO HE CONSIDERED A VULGAR PLAGIARIST — HE WAS INTERVIEWED ON "DATELINE N.B.C." WHERE HE SAID I WAS LIVING IN A DREADFUL HOTEL — MY LITTLE ROOM IN THAT HOTEL MEANT HOME TO ME & I WAS SO PROUD OF MYSELF — MR. HARRISON WOULDN'T LAST TEN MINUTES ON THE STREET & WOULD SWOON IF HE WAS IN JAIL — HE'S A GROUPIE —

— 2003 — WATCHED THE ACADEMY AWARDS ON TV — WHAT I SAW WAS EXALTED MEDIOCRITY — WHAT I DID NOT SEE WAS GENIUS — ORIGINALITY — TEMPERAMENT — IT'S LATE & I'M GOING TO WALK MY DOG —

— 90'S – WOKE UP ONE MORNING WITH CHEST PAINS – AS USUAL MONEY WAS SCARCE – SO TAKING THE EIGTH AV. BUS & ARRIVING IN THE EMERGENCY ROOM WAS MY WAY OF GETTING TO THE HOSPITAL – WINDING UP IN INTENSIVE CARE & PLACED ON THE CRITICAL LIST – THEY CALLED MY CHILDREN WITH THE NEWS – MY DAUGHTER FLEW DOWN FROM NEW ENGLAND TO BE WITH ME – MY SON WAS WORKING IN PARIS & CALLED ME – WAS THERE FOR SIX DAYS – THEY NEVER WASHED ME OR CHANGED LINEN – BEING A SENIOR CITIZEN WITH MEDICARE DOSEN'T MEAN YOU ARE A HUMAN BEING TO THESE IDIOTS – MY DAUGHTER RAISED HELL & WAS IGNORED – SHE TOOK ME HOME ON DAY SIX WHERE I COULD SHOWER & SLEEP I "ME OWN BED" –

— 60'S ME & A NORMA & THREE YEAR OLD

TERRY TOOK A TWO WEEK VACATION IN MOROCCO — STAYED AT BEST HOTEL IN TANGIER — SCORED SOME HASHISH FROM AHMED AKBAR — THE DEALER FOR THE STONES — TOOK MY SON ON MY BACK EVERY MORNING IN THE HOTEL POOL — LOTS OF FASHIONISTAS + EUROTRASH POOLSIDE — WE WOULD TAXI TO A DESERTED BEACH CALLED 'MIAMI' + WATCHED CAMEL CARAVANS CROSSING THE DESERT — DINNER LATE AT NIGHT AT THE TOP OF THE CASBAH — MY WIFE + ME WERE DRIFTING —

= 80'S — SAN FRACISCO IS NOT NEW YORK (NO CITY IS) BUT IT IS ONE OF MY FAVORITE PLACES — IT'S NO SURPRISE THAT EUROPEANS LIKE IT — IF YOU LIVE THERE YOU REALISE THIS IS "SEX CITY" — IT'S IN THE AIR — IT'S IN THE WATER — IT'S ON THE STREET — THE TOURISTS ARE THE ONLY ONES WHO ARE NOT SCORING SEX — THEY ARE THE ONES WHO

WALK THE HILLS ON COLD SUMMER DAYS WEARING T SHIRTS THAT SAY "MALIBU" —

— 80'S — GOT A JOB AS A TELEPHONE NUISANCE SELLING THE S.F. CHRONICLE — SIX DAYS A WEEK — FOUR NUMBING HOURS EACH DAY — MAKING ENOUGH FOR RENT + FOOD — NOW HOOKED ON RED WINE — READ THE PAPER EVERY DAY — NEVER LOOKED AT A MAGAZINE — FASHION PHOTOGRAPHY AS AN ART FORM WAS BEING DESTROYED — GOT A HOT PLATE + COOKED ONE COURSE MEALS FOR MYSELF — WAS VERY GRATEFUL FOR THIS FOOD + BOOZE — MY EX WIFE WAS THE ONLY ONE WHO KNEW WHERE I WAS — CALLED HER TO SEE IF MY SON WAS O.K. — GOT THE FEELING THAT HER SECOND MARRIAGE WAS FALLING APART —

— 90'S — ONE NIGHT TERRY'S WIFE NIKKI CALLED TO TELL ME THAT

MY SON HATED ME — HE DIDN'T HATE ME — HE HATED HER — LATER ON HE DIVORCED HER WHILE SHE WAS RECOVERING FROM BREAST CANCER — A MAN NEVER LEAVES A WOMAN HE LOVES — TERRY FALLS IN LOVE EVERY FULL MOON —

— 2003 — TRYING TO ORGANISE AN EXHIBIT AT A "NEW HOLLYWOOD" GALLERY — THE OPENING IS NEXT WEEK — NOT A PHOTOGRAPHY SHOW — HAVE DESIGNED THIRTY POSTERS THAT USE PHOTOGRAPHS THAT ARE DIGITALLY REPRODUCED PLUS COPY (QUOTES — COMMENTS) THIS IS THE FIRST GRAPHIC DESIGN JOB THAT I'VE DONE SINCE THE 50'S — VERY PLEASED WITH THE RESULTS — POSTER ART IS A VERY OLD ART FORM — ADORE THE WORD "DIGITAL" — HOPE THEY SELL BECAUSE MORE POVERTY AWAITS — I HAVE A GOD GIVEN TALENT + IT'S ALL ONE NEEDS — IS "NEW HOLLYWOOD" READY FOR BOB RICHARDSON —

— 2003 — WRITING THIS IS GETTING EASIER — ONCE YOU STRIP YOURSELF NAKED IN FRONT OF THE WHOLE WORLD YOU BETTER HAVE A NICE DICK —

— 2003 — JUST GOT A CALL FROM GALLERY OWNER WHO IS A HUSTLER — TIRED OF BEING LIED TO — I CANCELED THE SHOW — TOO BAD BECAUSE I LIKE THE POSTERS — SOMETHING ELSE WILL COME THROUGH — GOOD OR BAD SOMETHING ALWAYS COMES — TO SURVIVE — HAVING FAITH IN MYSELF + IN GOD HAS TAKEN ME HERE — MAYBE IT'S TIME TO MOVE — BUT MOVE WHERE —

— 2003 — THE GALLERY OWNER + HIS PUBLICIST CALLED TO APOLOGIZE — MORE LIES — BUT THERE IS A NEW DATE SET FOR THE END OF THIS MONTH — AS USUAL — NEEDING MONEY — THIS SHOW BETTER HAPPEN —

- 70's — WAS ABLE TO SAVE ENOUGH MONEY TO BUY A YAMAHA MOTORSCOOTER — THERE HAVE TO BE MORE BIKES + SCOOTERS IN S.F. THAN ANY OTHER CITY — INCLUDING ROME —

- 80's — MY SON CALLED + WANTED TO VISIT — HE BROUGHT SOME FASHION PHOTOGRAPHS TO SHOW ME — THEY WERE NOT GOOD — TELLING HIM SO WAS NOT DIFFICULT — WHEN SLAMMED IN THE FACE WITH THE TRUTH HE REACTED THE WAY HIS FATHER WOULD — THE SIMPLE TRUTH IS THE ONLY WAY TO WORK WITH KIDS — I TOLD HIM THAT SEX + VIOLENCE WOULD BE USED BY ALL THE ARTS — MAYBE MOVING TO ~~NY~~ S.F. WOULD HELP HIM —

  - 80's — ALL THESE YEARS IN S.F. ENABLED ME TO SAVE MYSELF — SCHIZOPHRENIC ATTACKS STOPPED — YOU MUST — HOWEVER — BE ON GUARD.

EVERY DAY YOU STUDY THE WORLD AROUND YOU — NO MORE VOICES — NO MORE HALLUCINATIONS — IT TOOK YEARS OF GOING TO WORK EVERY MORNING — A CLEVER MONKEY COULD DO THE WORK I DID — BUT IT CALMED ME — TAKING CARE OF MYSELF — NEVER ASKING FOR HELP — WAS MY ROAD TO "CURE" —

— 90'S — THE EDITOR OF ITALIAN VOGUE FANCIES HERSELF AS AN EMPRESS — SHE AIN'T NO DIANA VREELAND — SHE HAD A DINNER PARTY AT THE MILLER GALLERY — ALL THE FASHION VICTIMS WERE INVITED — PLUS ELTON JOHN — MARYANN FAITHFULL ETC. — I DIDN'T SHOW UP — I HAVE NOTHING IN COMMON WITH THESE NITWITS — THIS LITTLE EDITOR + HER ART DIRECTOR BOYFRIEND STARTED TAKING PAGES AWAY FROM ME + GIVING THEM TO THE PHOTOGRAPHERS WHO KISS HER ASS — "GOLDILOCKS ON ACID" IS HOW I SEE THIS LITTLE BROAD —

— 80'S — WHILE SHOPPING AT MACYS IN S.F. SOMETHING GOOD HAPPENED — WENT PAST THEIR CAMERA DEPT. + SAW A SIGN READING "POINT + SHOOT" — THERE IN A DISPLAY CASE WAS A TINY RICOH — TOTALLY AUTOMATIC — NOTHING TO DO BUT PRESS THE SHUTTER BUTTON — STARTED SAVING — BUT WHAT WOULD I SHOOT — ALL THE MEMORIES OF A TWENTY YEAR BATTLE TO GET MY WORK PUBLISHED CAME HOME — BUT THERE WERE LANDSCAPES — SHOULD I TRY —

— 80'S — GETTING UP AT DAWN EVERY MORNING TO SHOOT THE FOG + THE BEAUTIFUL EMPTY STREETS — THE CAMERA PRODUCED IMAGES THAT WOWED ME — KNOWING HOW EASY IT WOULD BE TO SHOOT EVEN FASHION PHOTOGRAPHS STARTED SOMETHING IN ME THAT KEPT ME AWAKE AT NIGHT — DRINKING "DAGO RED" + SMOKING CIGARETTES I REALISED WHAT I FELT WAS HOPE —

80'S — BECOMING THE VERY BEST PHOTOGRAPHY TEACHER ON THIS PLANET HAPPENED WITH A SON WHO WANTED MONEY & FAME & GOT IT — FAME NEVER HAPPENED TO ME — DOES SUCCESS MAKE A MAN HAPPY — YES — BUT IT ALSO MAKES A MAN LONELY — NEVER UNDERSTANDING WHETHER SOMEONE WANTS TO KNOW YOU OR JUST WANTS TO BE ANOTHER MOTH AROUND YOUR FLAME — GOING BEYOND FAME WAS ~~WHAT~~ MY GOAL — AND IT HAPPENED — ANYONE WHO IS CONSIDERED A LEGEND PAYS A HEAVY PRICE — TERRY WAS LIVING IN L.A. — HE WOULD SEND ME HIS CONTACT SHEETS — EDITING THEM & MAILING THEM FROM S.F. WAS NOT WORKING — HE MOVED UP TO S.F. — WHERE WE WOULD WORK EVERY DAY FOR A LONG TIME — HE IS STILL THE BEST & LEAST GRATEFUL OF ALL MY STUDENTS —

— 2003 — SPENT YESTERDAY GETTING SMASHED WITH A CLOSE FRIEND — TOO BAD ANGER IS PART OF LOVE — IF YOU ARE PASSIONATE — YOU ARE NOT GOING TO HAVE EASY RELATIONSHIPS = IF SOMEONE HIDES THEIR "DARK SIDE" — YOU DO NOT KNOW THEM — IF YOU CAN NOT LIVE WITH THE TRUTH ABOUT YOURSELF — YOU HAVE NOTHING TO GIVE — TODAY IS CLEAR + I CAN SEE THE SAN GABRIEL MOUNTAINS CHANGING COLOR —

— 2003 — PEACE BEGINS AT THE END OF EVERY WAR —

— 2003 — MUSLIM WOMEN REMIND ME OF NUNS — NO MAKEUP — COVERED FROM HEAD TO FOOT — WALKING BEHIND THE SUPERIOR MALE —

— 2003 — IT DOESN'T MATTER HOW THE WORLD SEE'S YOU — THE ONLY THING THAT COUNTS IS WHAT YOUR MIRROR TELL'S YOU =

- 70'S — THERE WAS A YOUNG MAN WHO LIVED ON THE BEACH NEAR ME — SOMETIMES I WOULD TALK TO HIM ABOUT HIS LIFE — STRICKEN WITH SCHITZOPHRENIA WHILE IN COLLEGE — HE WAS NOT DIAGNOSED PROPERLY — BRILLIANT — WITH BEAUTIFUL MANNERS — HE WAS COVERED WITH DIRT — HE WAS A GRADUATE OF HARVARD LAW SCHOOL — HIS WEALTHY FAMILY ABANDONED HIM —

- 90'S — WROTE TO THE EDITORS OF HARPER'S BAZHAR & FRENCH VOGUE ASKING FOR AN ASSIGNMENT — THEY IGNORED ME — WHERE & HOW WERE THESE "LADIES" BRAUGHT UP — A SIMPLE NOTE SAYING NO WOULD HAVE BEEN CIVILIZED — AT SOME POINT ALL MAGAZINE EDITORS ARE FIRED —

- 2003 — THE TIMES HAD A PIECE RECENTLY ABOUT PHIL SPECTOR SAYING HE WAS SCHITZOPHRENIC — MOZART WOULD ADORE THE "WALL OF SOUND" —

- 2003 — HOW ABSURD LIFE IS —

- 2003 — ACTORS COMPLAIN THAT HOLLYWOOD TURNS EVERYONE INTO A WHORE — THAT MEANS THAT ALL THESE PATHETIC "CELEBRITIES" ARE WHORES — NO WONDER MOST AMERICAN FILMMAKERS ARE PANDERING — WHAT DO WHORES SEE IN THEIR MIRRORS —

- 30'S — HAVING TWO SURGERIES (HERNIA & APPENDIX) FOR A CHILD CAN BE HELL — HOW MANY TIMES IN MY LIFE HAVE I WANTED TO GO HOME — TO ESCAPE BEING A VICTIM OF THESE SOULLESS PEOPLE.

- 2003 — DESIGNING POSTERS FOR AN EXHIBIT HAS SHOWN ME WHAT A GOOD GRAPHIC DESIGNER BOB RICHARDSON IS — ART DIRECTING BOOKS OR A MAGAZINE WOULD MAKE ME JOYFUL — HATE THE EXPRESSION CREATIVE DIRECTOR — LOW WOULD KNOW HOW PHONY THAT SOUNDS

IF YOU HAD STUDIED WITH ALEXI BRODOVITCH + WORKED WITH DIANA VREELAND — THEY MADE THE MAGAZINE'S EDITORIAL PAGES WORKS OF ART — BOTH WERE ARISTOCRATIC + TEMPERMENTAL — THEY WERE ORIGINAL + AT THE END BOTH OF THEM WERE BADLY TREATED — MAYBE CHANEL WAS CORRECT ABOUT AMERICAN FASHION EDITORS —

— 30'S — MY MOTHER WAS A "FLAPPER" IN THE TWENTIES — THERE ARE PHOTOGRAPHS OF HER IN MY FAMILY ALBUM TAKEN IN THE THIRTIES ~~ALONG~~ ALONG WITH MY FATHER THAT I HAVE REPRODUCED ~~OFF~~ MANY TIMES — SHE TOLD US THAT SHE SMOKED + DRANK GIN WHEN IT WAS FROWNED ON — IN SOME OF THESE PICTURES HER HAIR I CUT LIKE A BOY — WHEN SHE + MY FATHER WOULD DANCE FOR US SHE WOULD "SHIMMY" — YOU DO NOT FORGET BEING TOLD THAT IT WAS IMPORTANT TO BE A "STRONG LEAD" —

— 70'S — I AM HAUNTED BY my FATHER — ALL OF THE CHILDISH CONFUSION — ALL OF THE ENVY FOR MY DOOMED OLDER BROTHER VANISHED YEARS AGO — TELLING MY SON THAT WATCHING OVER HIM — HAUNTING HIM AFTER MY DEATH MAKES HIM SMILE — SOME DAY HE WILL ASK HIMSELF — WHEN FREIGTENED OR CONFUSED — "WHAT WOULD MY DAD TELL ME TO DO" — KNOWING FINALLY THAT THERE IS A RIGHT + A WRONG IS A COMFORT — YOU MUST FOLLOW YOUR INSTINCS THE WAY ALL ANIMALS DO —

— 90'S — THE NEW YORKER DESCRIBED ME AS VOLATILE — IS THERE AN ARTIST WHO IS PASSIONATE ABOUT HIS WORK — ANYWHERE ON EARTH — WHO ISN'T VOLATILE — THE WRITER OF THAT PIECE IS TOO BUSY IN HER PURSUIT OF MAKING MONEY TO HAVE ANY TEMPERMENT — BESIDES MY HERITEGE IS IRISH —

— 80's — HAVING MOOVED TO SAN FRANCISCO TO WORK WITH ME — TERRY NOW GOT A CRASH COURSE IN PHOTOGRAPHY — HE SCOFFED AT THE IDEA OF USING A "POINT + SHOOT" CAMERA LIKE MINE + INSISTED ON A NIKON — HAVING BEEN ONE OF THE FIRST TO USE A NIKON TO SHOOT FASHION IN THE EARLY 60's — IT WAS THE SAME AS ALL SLOW CAMERAS TO ME — WITH A NIKON — BY THE TIME YOU READ THE LIGHT + FIND YOUR FOCUS — THE IMAGE YOU SAW IS GONE — FOR THE LAST THIRTEEN YEARS A POINT + SHOOT LEICA IS ALL I'VE USED —

— 2003 — HOLLYWOOD CELEBRITIES SEEM TO BE TERRIBLY PROUD OF BEING DÉCLASSÉ —

— 2003 — THE ONLY WAY TO SURVIVE LIFE IN THE 21ST CENTURY IS TO BE ABOVE IT ALL — WAY ABOVE —

— 60'S — BENEDETTA BARZINI WAS A "WILD CHILD" — THE DAUGHTER OF THE WRITER LUIGI BARZINI — SHE WAS ARISTOCRATIC + INTELLIGENT — DID A STORY WITH HER + POLLY MELLON (EDITOR) TOLD ME THEY HAD TO WASH HER FEET IN THE DRESSING ROOM — SHE WAS THIN + ATE A HUGE LUNCH — LATER SHE PICKED FOOD OUT OF THE GARBAGE — IRVING PENN — WHO SHE CONSIDERED A GENIUS — DID SUPERB PICTURES OF HER — SHE CLAIMED DICK AVEDON WAS A PHONY — THE ONLY "WILD CHILD" TODAY IS KATE MOSS —

— 60'S — LESBIANS — WHO ARE LIKE BEAUTIFUL MEN — FASCINATE ME — SO MANY PHOTOGRAPHS OF MINE DURING THIS PERIOD WOULD SHOW INTAMCY BETWEEN TWO WOMEN — TODAY PHOTOGRAPHERS DO UGLY PHOTOS OF HARD CORE : "DYKES" — I'VE WORKED WITH SOME FASHION EDITORS IN PARIS WHO WERE "LESBIAN CHIC" THEMSELVES — PEGGY ROCHE (ELLE) WAS THE BEST —

— 60'S — DID PICTURES IN ARLES — WHERE VAN GOUGH PAINTED — THE LIGHT WAS BRILLIANT — WILD ARABIAN HORSES RUNNING FREE — I WORKED WITH A BEAUTIFUL YOUNG FRENCH GIRL WHO BECAME A HEROIN ADDICT + HAD TO HAVE HER ARM AMPUTATED —

— 60'S — ANITA PALENBERG WAS BEYOND WILD — WE DID A STORY FOR "TWEN" — AN AVANT GARDE GERMAN MAGAZINE — SHOOTING "RICH HIPPIE" PHOTOS BECAME MY THING FOR A SHORT TIME — BEING ONE OF THEM MADE IT TOO EASY — ANITA'S SON MARLON (WITH KEITH RICHARDS) IS A FRIEND OF TERRYS — AN ENGLISH EDITOR RECENTLY GAVE ME A MESSAGE FROM ANITA WHO IS A STYLIST IN LONDON — ANITA WAS ONE OF THE STARS OF "PERFORMANCE" —

— 2003 — THE MOST PATHETIC PEOPLE ARE "SELF HATING AMERICANS" — HOW STUPID — HOW UNGRATEFUL —

— 2003 — LOOKING BACK + REALISING THAT ~~I AM~~ I AM NEVER LONELY WHEN I AM BY MYSELF — MY BEST PHOTOGRAPHS ARE OF LONELY WOMEN — MEN + CHILDREN — RECENTLY SHOT THORA BIRCH WHO TOLD ME SHE COULD NOT ACT OUT LONELINESS — BUT SHE COULD ACT OUT BEING ALONE — MY WAY OF WORKING WITH HOLLYWOOD ACTORS IS — "SHUT UP + DO AS YOU'RE TOLD" —

— 2003 — AMERICA HAS BECOME A NATION OF PERFORMERS — RATHER THAN BEING THEMSELVES THEY ARE PRETENDING TO BE SOMEONE ACCEPTABLE — ANDY WAS RIGHT —

— 2003 — IT SHOULD BE AGAINST THE LAW FOR AMERICANS TO USE THE WORD "SEXY" FOR AT LEAST TEN YEARS —

— 80'S — TERRY WOULD GO TO THE GAP STORE ON MARKET STREET +

BUY CLOTHES — SHOOT THEM ON LOCAL MODELS — BRING THEM BACK TO THE STORE — PROCESS THE FILM & I WOULD EDIT IT & DO LAYOUTS FOR HIM — IT TOOK ABOUT A YEAR TO PUT TOGETHER A BEAUTIFUL PORTFOLIO — HE WAS GETTING READY TO GO TO NEW YORK — SHOULD I FOLLOW — WOULD ANYONE WORK WITH ME — 15 YEARS IS A LONG TIME TO BE AMONG THE MISSING & PRESUMED DEAD — THEN MARTIN HARRISON'S BOOK CAME OUT —

— 2003 — THE GALLERY SHOW OF THIRTY POSTERS THAT I DESIGNED IS SCHEDULED FOR LATER THIS MONTH — MY FAVORITE WORD IS "DIGITAL" — THEY'LL BE A BAR & A DISK JOCKEY & I'LL PROVIDE THE C.D.'S — ALL LONELY & HAUNTING NEW MUSIC — I WILL BE THE YOUNGEST PERSON IN A GALLERY FULL OF 20 YEAR OLDS —

— 2003 — MALE POLITICIANS ARE IN A BATTLE TO SEE WHO CAN BE THE BIGGEST BITCH —

— 2003 — DOWN THE ROAD FROM ME THERE'S A RAVISHING JACARANDA TREE — IT WILL BLOSSOM SOON WITH MAUVE FLOWERS —

— 80'S — TERRY AND ME — FATHER + SON — WHEN WILL HE BE MAN ENOUGH TO ASK ME FOR MY SIDE OF THE STORY — HE WAS TOLD THAT HIS FATHER ABANDONED HIM & HE BOUGHT IT — A FRIEND OF HIS TOLD ME THAT HE NEVER STOPS BAD MOUTHING ME — HE REMINDS ME OF MY OLDER BROTHER — ANOTHER BULLY —

— 80'S — TERRY GOES TO NEW YORK — COULD I PHOTOGRAPH AGAIN — HE HAS CONVINCED ME OF ONE THING — TEACHING PHOTOGRAPHY IS SECOND NATURE — READY OR NOT — HERE I COME — BACK FROM THE DEAD —

- 2003 - HOLLYWOOD CELEBRITIES ARE NOT ARROGANT - THEY ARE STUPID -

- 90'S - CAME HOME TO MY NEW YORK - ARRIVING AT NIGHT - STAYING WITH A HOSTILE TERRY - MY OLD MODEL DONNA MITCHEL ASKED HER NEW "BEST FRIEND" STEVEN MEISEL TO CALL SCHOOL OF VISUAL ART ON MY BEHALF - IT TOOK HIM TWO MONTHS TO CALL THEM - BUT THEY HIRED ME TO TEACH A CLASS - DICK AVEDON WAS TEACHING AT INTERNATIONAL CENTER OF PHOTOGRAPHY + GOT ME A TEACHING GIG THERE - ONE OF MY STUDENTS WAS AMY ARBUS (DIANE'S KID) - S.V.A. HAS BAD TEACHERS + GOOD STUDENTS - I ADOPT ALL MY STUDENTS - THE TEACHERS CAN'T FACE THE TRUTH - BUT THE STUDENTS CAN - THANK GOD FOR FEROCIOUS KIDS - LIVING ON SOCIAL SECURITY + TEACHER'S PAY - AS USUAL NO MONEY -

- 90'S - TERRY DISCOVERS THE "POINT + SHOOT" CAMERA - HE ONLY USES IT ON MAGAZINE WORK - HE DOES A BIG PERFORMANCE WHEN HE DOES ADVERTISING WORK - USING A BIGGER CAMERA - ASSISTANTS + STUDIO HELP ALL DOING THEIR BEST TO "GRAB THE MONEY + RUN" -

- 2003 - GLARING SUNSHINE TODAY - SMOG HIDING THE MOUNTAINS - WHEN IS THE NEXT BIG EARTHQUAKE COMING - IF L.A. FLOATS OUT INTO THE PACIFIC OCEAN - I CHOOSE NOT TO BE ABORD -

- 90'S - TERRY MOVES TO EAST VILLAGE + LAUNCHES HIS OWN CAMPAIN TOWARD FAME + FORTUNE - EDITING HIS WORK IS WHAT I HAVE BEEN ASSIGNED - ONE DAY HE THREW A METAL CHAIR AT ME - JUST MISSING MY HEAD - HE IGNORES THE FACT THAT HIS FATHER IS STILL RECOVERING -

➤ 90'S — MEET THE PUBLISHER OF "BIG" MAGAZINE — TURN DOWN SMALL ASSIGNMENT — DEMAND THE WHOLE ISSUE — COVER TO COVER — I WOULD DO NEW PHOTOGRAPHY — DO THE LAYOUTS + WRITE THE TEXT — TO MY AMAZEMENT HE AGREES — FOR THE NEXT FOUR MONTHS I SHOT THE ISSUE WITH A POINT + SHOOT LEICA I BORROWED — NO PHOTOGRAPHER HAS EVER SHOT THE ENTIRE ISSUE OF A MAGAZINE WITH ONE BORROWED CAMERA — AND SO THE LEGEND GROWS — TERRY IS DRIFTING AWAY — STILL CONTROLLED BY HIS MOTHER —

➤ 90'S — WORKING ON MOST SECTIONS OF BIG — ROAMING MY NEW YORK — KIDS IN THE SUBWAY — BARREN WINTERTIME CONEY ISLAND — DOING LANDSCAPES — STILL LIFES — SMALL CHILDREN — NUDE STRAIGHT MEN — MEN'S + WOMEN'S FASHION — I WAS DETERMINED TO DO ALL ONE CAN DO WITH A CAMERA —

— 2003 — THE FASHION INDUSTRY & THE ENTERTAINMENT INDUSTRY ARE A PERFECT MARRIAGE — BOTH ARE TRYING TO ELEVATE MEDIOCRITY — POOR DARLINGS HAVE FORGOTTEN THAT DIVORCE IS ALWAYS A PART OF ACT THREE —

— 50'S — THE CHILDREN IN KOREA HAUNT ME — STANDING ON THE SIDE OF THE ROAD BEGGING FOR CHOCOLATE FROM THE "G.I.'S" — ONE CHILD HAD LOST HER LEFT EYE & HER EYELID HAD BEEN PULLED DOWN & STICHED TO HER CHEEK — HAVE NEVER FORGOTTEN HER HOLDING OUT HER LITTLE HANDS FOR SOMETHING TO EAT — PIZZA PARLORS IN L.A. — WHEN TALKING TO THE KOREAN OWNERS ONE GETS THE FEELING THEY WANT TO FORGET — BIG MISTAKE — THE LAST TIME BLACK PEOPLE WENT ON A RAMPAGE IN L.A. THEY TARGETED KOREAN BUSINESS OWNERS — MORE BULLIES —

— 90'S — DICK AVEDON INTRODUCED ME TO THE STALEY WISE GALLERY IN NEW YORK + THE FAHEY KLINE GALLERY IN L.A. — HE INSISTED THEY REPRESENT ME — I HAD THE FEELING NONE OF THEM HAD EVER HEARD OF ME — STALEY WISE GAVE ME AN EXIBIT OF THE WORK COMPLETED FOR BIG MAGAZINE — THANK GOD FOR DICK AVEDON —

— 90'S — WITH TERRY'S HELP — ONCE AGAIN — MOVED TO SMALL PLACE IN HELL'S KITCHEN — IT WAS THE LAST TIME HE HAD TO HELP ME — A FORMER GHETTO FOR IRISH + ITALIAN IMIGRANTS — HELL'S KITCHEN BECAME MY FAVORITE LOCATION SITE —

— 90'S — SENT A COPY OF BIG TO FRANCA SOZZANI AT ITALIAN VOGUE — GRACIA D'ANUNZIO INTERVIEW ME + WE BECAME FRIENDS — MARIO SORRENTI WAS ASKED TO PHOTOGRAPH ME — MARIO IS BRILLIANT + A

GOOD MAN — HE IS "MOLTO ITALIANO" + AN ORIGINAL — SOZZANI KILLED THE PHOTOGRAPHS + ASKED ME TO DO TEN PAGES OF SELF PORTRAITS — SOZZANI ALSO ARRANGED FOR ME TO SHOOT A SMALL ADVERTISING CAMPAIGN FOR ALBERTO BIANNI — ALBERTO MADE AN ENTIRE WARDROBE FOR ME AS A GIFT — HAVING LIVED IN RAGS FOR TWO YEARS — THIS ITALIAN GESTURE MEANT MUCH TO ME — CIAO ALBERTO —

— 2003 — WHEN TWO CIVILIZATIONS COLLIDE — THE STRONGEST WILL PREVAIL — THERE IS NO STRONGER WEAPON ON THIS PLANET THAN CAPITALISM — IT SEEMS TO BE THE MOST FRIGHTENING TOO — SOMETIMES PEOPLE HAVE TO BE BROUGHT KICKING + SCREAMING INTO THIS CENTURY —

— 2003 — "THE BIGGER THEY ARE — THE HARDER THEY FALL" — THIS OLD CHESTNUT APPLIES TO THE

FASHION & ENTERTAINMENT GANGS — IT IS NOT WISE TO ALLOW PEOPLE TO PUT YOU ON A PEDESTEL — THINK OF ALL THE "MIGHTIE" IN NEW YORK & HOLLYWOOD WHO HAVE MADE THAT MISTAKE — THE FASHION MAGAZINES ALMOST ALWAYS FIRE EDITORS — USUALLY IN A VICIOUS — LOW CLASS WAY — IN HOLLYWOOD THEY DESTROY CAREERS IN ORDER TO PROTECT THEIR OWN — FEAR & INTIMIDATION RUN BOTH INDUSTRIES — A WHORE IN PRADA IS STILL A WHORE —

— 2003 — HAVE YOU SEEN THE ~~QUEEN~~ OUR LADY OF THE ANGELS CATHEDRAL IN DOWTOWN L.A. — THE EXTERIOR LOOKS LIKE A RATHER "SMART" PRISON — THE INTERIOR IS PURE LAS VEGAS — THE DOORS LOOK LIKE THE FAMOUS DOORS ON A CATHEDRAL IN FLORENCE — THIS EDIFICE COST MILLIONS & IS CLOSE BY POOR MEXICANS & THOUSANDS OF HUNGRY HOMELESS — YOU CAN SEE IT FROM THE HOLLYWOOD FREEWAY — HOW ~~ABSURD~~ FITTING —

⇒ 90'S — ALDO PRIMOLI — THE EDITOR OF L'UOMO VOGUE GAVE ME FOURTY PAGES IN ONE ISSUE — ALDO IS A BRILLIANT EDITOR WHO DOESN'T PLAY GAMES — HE KNOWS HOW TO WORK WITH PHOTOGRAPHERS ⇒ HIS BOSS WAS LITTLE MS. SOZZANI — GRACIA TOLD ME SHE DIDN'T LIKE ALDO + EVENTUALLY SHE GOT RID OF HIM — GRACIA TRIED HARD TO MAKE ME A PART OF THIS LITTLE SNAKE PIT — BUT I REFUSED ⇒ MY FATHER TAUGHT ALL OF US TO "NEVER MIX BUISNESS WITH PLEASURE" — IF YOU ARE A FASHION PHOTOGRAPHER — DOING BEAUTIFUL PICTURES SHOULD BE ENOUGH — ELLEN VON UNWERTH TOLD ME THAT YOU HAVE TO PLAY THE "GAME", HOW PATHETIC — ITALIAN VOGUE NEEDS A MEDICI —

⇒ 2003 — WHEN YOU ASK A "CREATIVE DIRECTOR" — WHAT HAVE YOU DONE THAT IS TRULY CREATIVE — YOU GET A BLANK STARE AS AN ANSWER —

- 2003 – TERRY'S BIG INFLUENCE IS LARRY CLARK – MR. CLARK IS NOW MENTORING A YOUNG GAY PHOTOGRAPHER WHOSE WORK IS INFLUENCED BY TERRY RICHARDSON – "WHAT GOES AROUND – COMES AROUND" –

- 90'S – TERRY IS BEING INTERVIEWED CONSTANTLY – HE SPENDS HALF OF EACH INTERVIEW TELLING THE WORLD WHAT A TERRIBLE FATHER I AM – OBVIOUSLY HE THINKS HE IS A TERRIFIC SON – THIS IS WHAT HAPPENS TO A CHILD WHO LIVES IN A HOME FULL OF HATE + REVENGE –

- 2003 – WHERE IS THE WOMAN WHO HAUNTS MY DREAMS – BEING 75 MEANS THAT SHE HAS TO APPEAR SOON – GETTING MARRIED AGAIN WOULD BE PERFECT –

- 2003 – ACCORDING TO HETEROSEXUAL + HOMOSEXUAL PEOPLE THERE IS NO SUCH THING AS BISEXUALITY –

THEY BELIEVE YOU ARE STRAIGHT OR GAY — BECAUSE THEY ARE — MORE BULL SHIT — I HAVE KNOWN MANY BISEXUAL MEN + WOMEN — THEY DO NOT SPEND THEIR ENTIRE LIVES HAVING ONE KIND OF SEX — THEY DO NOT HAVE THOSE INHIBITIONS — GROW UP AMERICA —

2003, — L.A. IS A WONDERFUL PLACE TO LIVE AS LONG AS YOU HAVE FRIENDS FROM NEW YORK + EUROPE — IT'S A STRANGE FEELING TO BE A FOREIGNER IN YOUR OWN COUNTRY —

= 90'S — WENT TO THE HAMPTONS TO DO SOME PAGES FOR ITALIAN VOGUE — SHOOTING MILA JOVOVICH ON THE BEACH — HER BOYFRIEND OF THE MOMENT — MARIO SORRENTI — CAME TO WATCH ME WORK — AT THE END OF THE DAY HE TOLD ME HE LEARNED FROM WATCHING ME — MAJOR COMPLIMENT — "IT TAKES ONE TO KNOW ONE" —

— 90'S — DID A ONE NIGHT SLIDE SHOW WITH BLASTING ROCK MUSIC FOR YOUNG PHOTOGRAPHERS & FASHIONISTAS — IT WAS HELD IN A VAST SPACE IN CHELSEA — WAS FOLLOWED MONTHS LATER BY HELMUT NEWTON + THEN MELVIN SOKOLSKY — YOUNG PHOTOGRAPHERS ALWAYS ASK THE SAME QUESTION — "HOW CAN I BECOME FAMOUS" — MY ANSWER IS ALWAYS THE SAME — "YOU WORK YOUR ASS OFF" —

= 90'S — INGRID SISCHY (EDITOR OF INTERVIEW) CALLED ONE NIGHT — SHE WANTED TO DO A STORY ON ME FOR THE NEW YORKER — SHE TOLD ME SHE WAS "A LITTLE JEWISH LESBIAN" — WE KEPT MEETING IN CHEAP RESTERAUNTS — ONE NIGHT SHE CAME OVER + SAT ON THE FLOOR BETWEEN MY LEGS — THIS WAS "LITTLE LULU" LULU" DOING HER JOURNALIST ACT — AS EXPECTED THE PIECE WAS A "HATCET JOB" —

→ 2003 – TODAY IS EASTER SUNDAY – WHEN WE WERE YOUNG – NEW CLOTHES FOR EASTER MASS WERE A TRADITION – WE WERE GIVEN AN EASTER GIFT AS WELL – DINNER WAS AT 4 P.M. AND DESERT AT SUPPER LATER THAT NIGHT – SOMETIMES THERE WAS SNOW – + SPRING FLOWERS IN MY FATHER'S GARDEN – EVERY POSSIBLE WILD FLOWER IS BLOOMING NOW IN L.A. – HOW I MISS MY DIFFICULT FATHER –

→ 2003 – REPORT IN THE TIMES QUOTING TOM FORD (IN PARIS) SAYING HE WAS "EMBARRESED" TO BE AN AMERICAN – THERE ARE MANY AMERICAN'S – INCLUDING ME – WHO THINK MR. FORD IS AN EMBARREMENT – HE IS MAKING A FORTUNE ON THE BACKS OF YOUNG ASSISTANT DESIGNERS – THE FRENCH HATE HIM – ..

→ 2003 – IN THE NEAR FUTURE THE WORD "CELEBRITY" IS GOING TO BECOME A DIRTY WORD –

= 2003 - THE POSTER SHOW IS NOW AT THE HOLLYWOOD GALLERY - THE OPENING NIGHT PARTY WAS CROWDED - FOUR POSTERS SOLD - WOULD BE REAL HAPPY TO DO SOME MORE GRAPHIC WORK - IT'S SO EASY FOR ME - MANY YOUNG PEOPLE AT THE SHOW - ALL SMOKING WEED ON THE PATIO - THEIR COMMENTS ON MY WORK ARE VALUABLE = ALL MY WORK IS DONE FOR THEM - WAS TOLD MY WORK LOOKS LIKE THE WORK OF A YOUNG ARTIST - THERE IS A YOUNG BOY TRAPPED INSIDE A SEVENTY FIVE YEAR OLD BODY - "GENERATION Y" AMAZES ME - THEY ARE SUPER HIP + COMPLETELY UNSOPHISTICATED THIS GENERATION CARRIES GUNS =

= 90'S = LIVING IN HELL'S KITCHEN + WORKING IN NEW YORK IS WEARING ME DOWN - KEEP THINKING ABOUT L.A. - THIS TIME I'LL HAVE A HOME =

— 2003 — APATHY IS A CRIPPLING AMERICAN DISEASE — IT IS EPIDEMIC WITH THE MILLIONS OF LEMMINGS IN THIS ONCE STRONG COUNTRY — THE APATHETIC CAUSE AS MUCH HARM AS THE TERRORISTS — SILENCE CAN BE READ AS COMPLIANCE — AMERICA HAS BECOME A LIBERAL STATE OF "ALL TALK + NO ACTION" — HAVING AN OPINION IS TABOO —

— 90'S — NOT WORKING WITH ITALIAN VOGUE — SOZZANI WAS TAKING MY PAGES + GIVING THEM TO THE PHOTOGRAPHERS WHO KISS HER ASS — "HANGING OUT" WITH THESE FASHIONISTAS IS DULL — THEY THINK FASHION IS TRULY IMPORTANT — FASHION MAGAZINES WILL DIE A SLOW DEATH + BE REPLACED BY TECHNOLOGY — EVERY THING WILL BE REPLACED BY "TECHNO GOD'S" — WILL SEX BE INCLUDED —

— 90'S — BOUGHT A DIGITAL CAMCORDER — STARTED SHOOTING A DOCUMENTARY ON BOB RICHARDSON — WORKING FOR SIX MONTHS RECORDING MY LIFE — MY VIDEO FILM LOOKS EXACTLY LIKE MY STILL PHOTOS — THANK GOD FOR THIS SMALL TALENT I WAS BORN WITH —

— 2003 — IN THE FUTURE A FULL LENGTH MOVIE WILL BE MADE ON A COMPUTER —

— 2003 — FLIPPING THROUGH FASHION MAGAZINES IN THE SUPERMARKET IS SAD — WHAT I SEE IS COPYING + STEALING — TERRY WORRIES ME — HE SEEMS TOO SECURE — HE CONFUSES MONEY WITH SUCCESS — QUITTING AT THE TOP TERRIFIES HIM — HE SEEMS OBLIVIOUS TO THE IDEA THAT A YOUNG PHOTOGRAPHER WHO IS SHALLOW ENOUGH TO CRAVE FAME + MONEY MIGHT BE BEHIND HIM — WAITING FOR TERRY TO BECOME PASSÉ —

— 90'S — WHEN BEGINING TO WORK AGAIN BECAME A REALITY — PEOPLE LIKE BRUCE WEBER TOLD ME TO "BEHAVE" — WE COULD NEVER BE FRIENDS — PEOPLE WHO KNOW ME WOULD NEVER SAY ANYTHING SO CHILDISH —

— 2003 — MY ASSISTANT CALLED TO TELL ME THAT UNSIGNED PHOTOS BY BOB RICHARDSON ARE BEING SOLD ON "EBAY" FOR $500 EACH — THE SELLER IS IDENTIFIED AS A RETIRED ART DIRECTOR FROM VOGUE — HOW DID HE GET MY NEGATIVES — I CAN'T PAY MY RENT & HE IS MAKING MONEY OFF MY TALENT — IS THIS OK WITH ANNA WINTOUR & GRACE CODDINGTON — WHY AM I NOT SURPRISED THAT THIS ART DIRECTOR WORKED FOR VOGUE —

— 2003 — THERE ARE TWO KINDS OF PEOPLE PEOPLE ON EARTH — THOSE WHO LIVE IN THE PAST & THOSE

WHO LIVE IN THE FUTURE —
WHICH ONE ARE YOU —

= 2003 — HOW HAVE I BEEN ABLE
TO SURVIVE FOR SEVENTY FIVE
YEARS — GUTS — WILLPOWER — PRIDE
I AM VERY PROUD OF MYSELF —
I AM NOT ASHAMED OF ANYTHING =
I HAVE NO SECRETS — I AM FREE —
WHAT ABOUT YOU =

— THE BEGINNING —

1990-05

1990-05

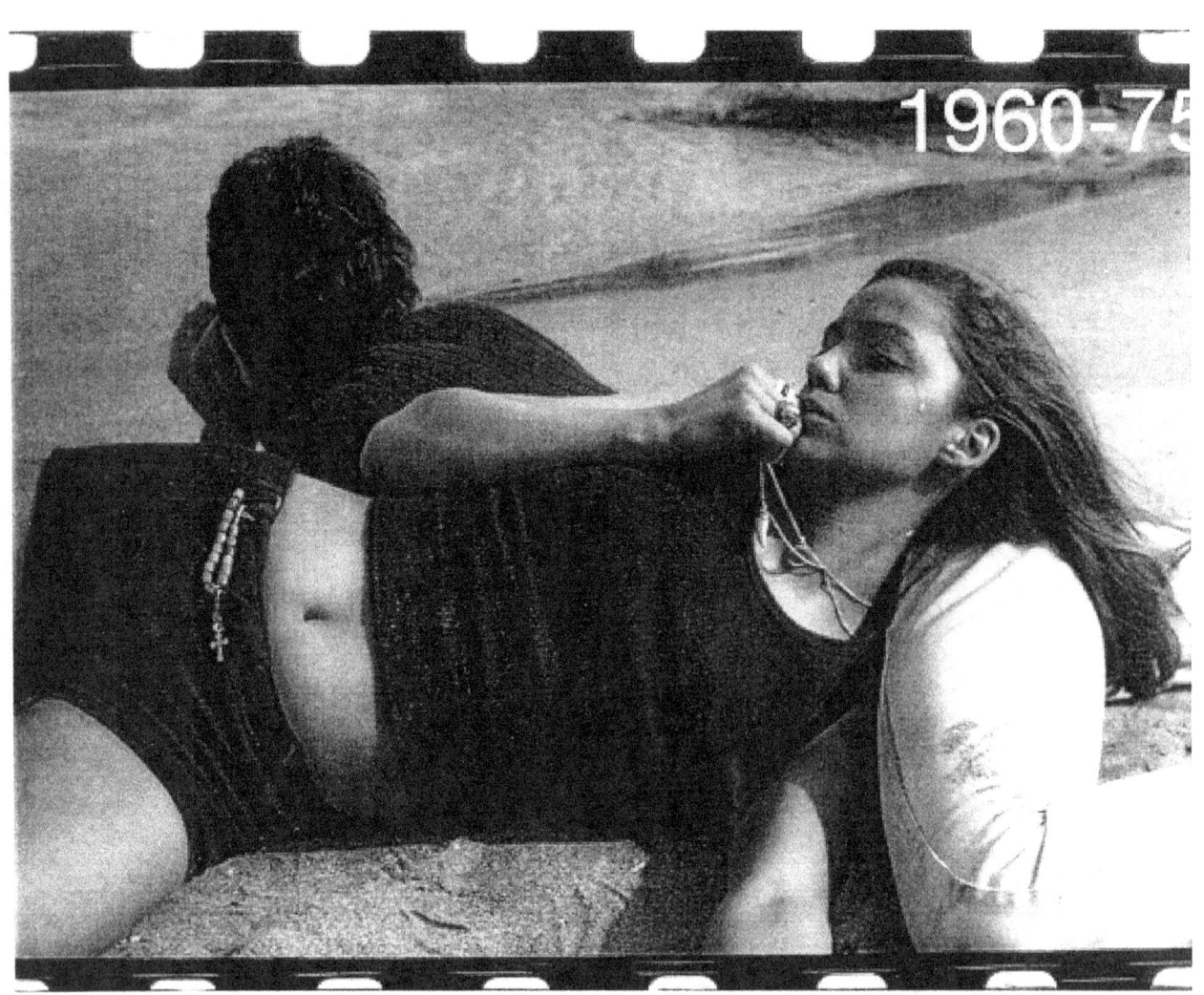

1960-7

1990-05

1990-05

1960-75

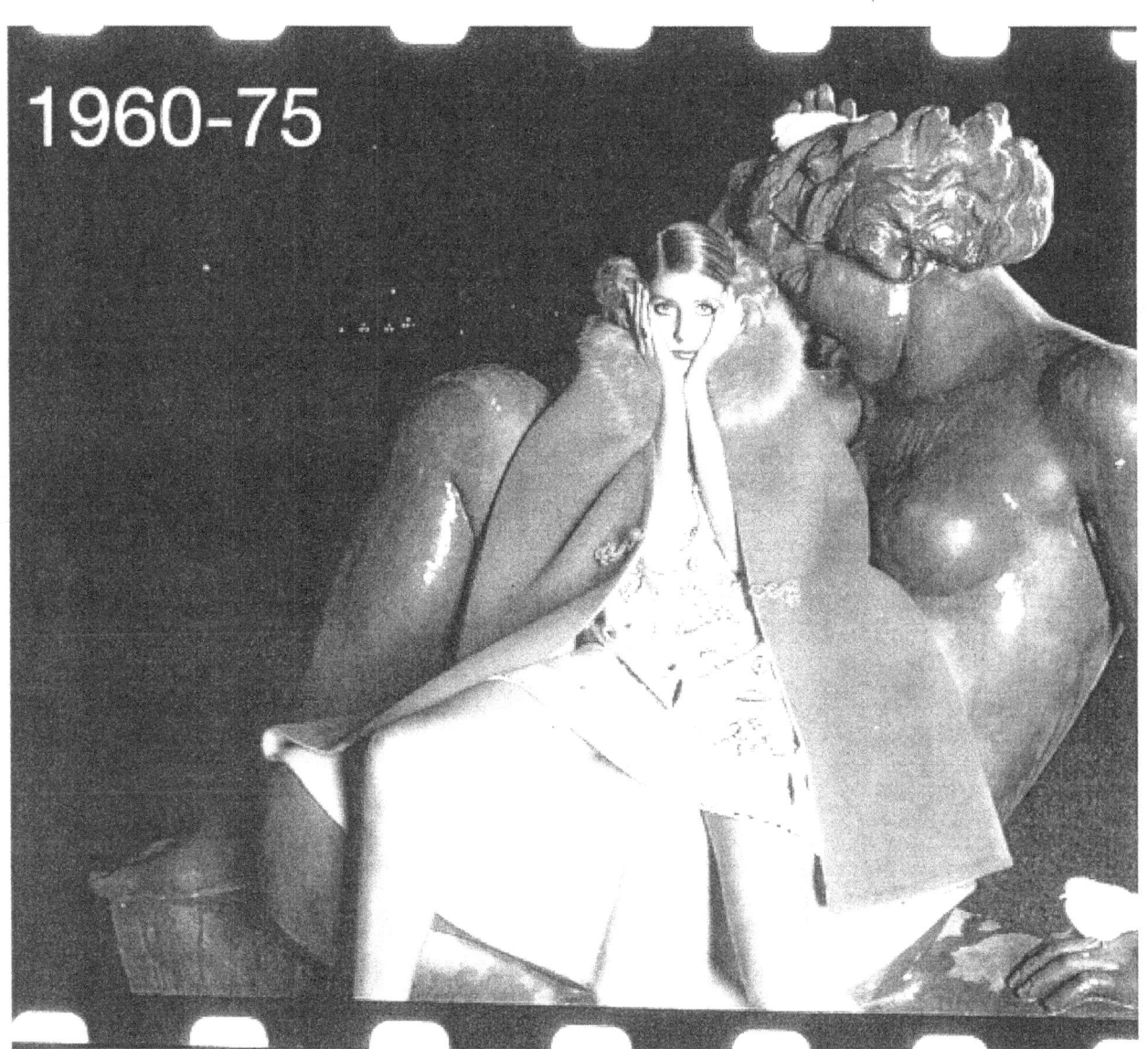

1960-75

www.ingramcontent.com/pod-product-compliance
Lightning Source LLC
Chambersburg PA
CBHW081228080526
44587CB00022B/3865